Yellow #5

J. Raymond

ISBN: 1979930333
ISBN-13: 978-1979930338

DEDICATION

To those no longer with me,
and my closest friends and family
stubborn and loving enough
who refuse to leave.

To Jesse
To Ellison
To my father, resting in peace
To my mother, still searching for it
To each and every one of you who,
in spite of myself and an insatiable urge to
continue pushing boundaries,
continue to support my art and worst habits.

Keep growing with me.

YELLOW #5 (also known as Tartrazine)

Tartrazine is a synthetic lemon yellow azo dye
primarily used as a food coloring.
Tartrazine is a commonly used color all over the
world, mainly for yellow. Products containing
tartrazine commonly include processed commercial
foods that have an artificial yellow or green
color, or that consumers expect to be brown or
creamy looking. It has been frequently used in the
bright yellow coloring of imitation "lemon"
filling in baked goods.

Rumors began circulating about tartrazine in the
1990s regarding a link to its consumption and
adverse effects on male potency, testicle and
penis size, and sperm count. There are no
documented cases supporting the claim tartrazine
will shrink a penis or cause it to stop growing.

A Letter To My Son

My words are silly little words. Often off putting. Vile. Gnawed on tongue-in-cheek. Words that, when we are older, will likely embarrass us both equally. If I said all these words were meant for you, it would be a lie. They aren't. They're mine. I'm selfish. Just ask your mother, she'll tell you so. She's usually spot on. Do yourself a favor and never forget to love her endlessly. In spite of everything. Angst, self-doubt, stubbornness or disagreements are no excuse. My words are dirty juvenile words. Hyperbolic. Cynical. Lacking in censoring. In desperate need of maturing. Words which never, ever encompass the depths of the love I feel for you. Some days, that's the absolute most difficult thing I'm forced to face. Some nights, I shut off all the lights in the house, just so I can better imagine your smile. My words fall short. These words never seem to close any of the distance between us. My words are nothing compared to you. One day, I will plead for an opportunity to explain myself. To explain why I left. I know that my reasons will sound like excuses. I accept that I'll have to find peace with moments missed out on, time I'll never get back, and the fact that I wasn't there when you needed me. My words will never make up for any of that. But maybe when you read this, it'll make sense. You'll see that in between these words, the spaces separating each sentence, the areas surrounding every page, are for you. They aren't empty. They aren't devoid of emotion. They are, merely, blank and waiting to be filled with a future I look forward to sharing with you. My words will be so much bigger then. More vivid. More apologetic. More of what you deserve. Not a day goes by where I'm not searching for those words. It's my life's work – you are my life's work. The greatest thing I'll ever create. And my days between now and then will be spent becoming someone I hope you'll be half as proud of, as I have always been of you, my son.

With all my love,

Jack

Peripheries

My fight has been mostly internal -
me against the world within myself.
And what comes easy for some
is war for others.
I am trying to appreciate whatever
and whoever
crosses my path, in the moment
and not only once it up and leaves.
To keep my eyes opened wide childlike,
take inventory of not merely what's in front of me,
but all those little unknowns
in the peripheries.
To not assume everyone is the enemy.

I watch how sunlight brightens one side of the street
yet can't stretch far enough to cross.
I should meet it half way,
seems simple enough.
Everyone over there looks mysterious
and all I want for
are their stories.
But only a few feet to my right
I notice a woman share a pint of soup with her dog
atop a cardboard box.
And I'm not nearly as afraid of them
as I am of those overflowing with purpose
and optimism.

You fall in love with the wrong things a few times
only to end up branded with lessons and lesions
you can't help but hide from.
I am trying to show you though.
To allow life to unfold,
and remind myself to control what I can.
Yet, there are things controlling me as well.

They laugh at my stubbornness and naiveté.
They tell me to loosen my grip,
put away my fists.
That I cannot punch my way out this.
That kindness and empathy and love
is what will ultimately save me from myself.

So, I struggle to uncover and give away the parts of me
that have never come naturally.
Take them while you can.

Forgive me when we can't.

Johnson & Whales

You ask bluntly if we can go somewhere.
I tell you to be more blunt.
"Let's fuck", is your response.
It's been a long day
a long month
a long life, already.
I am too tired to presume.
A half hour later, a salty ocean breeze blows against
my back and bare ass.
You are bent over a bench,
I can't even see your face.
While I'm redressing, I'm regressing.
Your phone rings as I tighten my belt into the second notch.

"Hey daddy",
you say innocently enough for us to feel guilty...
"I'm on my way home right now."

You are twenty-one and a half.
I am more than a decade deeper into this nonsense.
I am your fourteenth,
or some other irrelevant number perfect for a drunk
Wednesday evening.
You tell me "this was fun"
so casually that it's cutting.

This breeze is nice, but can't this matter?
I need this to be something significant.
It's what I do.
It's how I cope with the fact that I'm deprived,
going nowhere as slowly as possible,
taking far more than I'm ever giving in return.

It's what I do.
I try.

I try and get you to believe you deserve better
in general
overall
entirely
fuck......
I'm already sorry.
I'm already getting in the way of a moment,
I'm already ruining it/this.

You say you are content just being fucked,
happy to be wanted,
that it felt nice/right.
And I won't leave well enough alone.
I taste your underlying lies on my tongue
as I exhale cigarette smoke into the path
of a jogging passerby.
Five minutes earlier and he'd have stopped
to watch our charade.
Now, nothing.
It didn't matter to him either.
We were just two people walking to your red car on "E",
wishing we were something important enough to forget.
Or was that just me?

"Let me know you got home safely"
I say.
You won't, and that's ok as well.
At least I care enough to ask.
Even when it isn't nearly enough for you to believe
you mean something to someone
who cannot convince you otherwise.

Windowshills

We are forever blossoming and wilting
taking new roots in places we have never been before.

I am listening to old men tell bayou stories
of catfishing and crawfish hauling.
An old Western plays in the background
while grey dogs sleep loudly at our feet.
Anxious little girls grow up with grandparents,
are quick to show us oxidized photos
of how much they resemble a father
who doesn't come around here anymore.
Side-by-side smiles
and blue
overcast eyes
finding similarities shared
only they will ever see.

Hank Williams and Loretta Lynn show up
just before the afternoon storms roll in.
I'm lighting one cigarette after another,
laughing at how easy it was for you to tell me that
my time does not matter.
See,
I realized three days ago there was zero future with you.
So I used my last few dollars
to buy your mother a bouquet of flowers
then thanked her for her hospitality.

As often as I'm told to grow up, learn more quickly,
most of you are never enough
to fill these holes left in my chest.
I love fast enough to realize just as quickly
strangers can't fill voids left within me.

Just then,
a cardinal lands on her grandfather's windowsill,
and he believes it's his late wife.

Says that she visits him daily.

Understand what it is that I am saying…

He BELIEVES this wholeheartedly,
unquestionably
without reservation.
He wakes early to have coffee with her each morning.

I am reminded right then and there
that something heartbreakingly beautiful happens
when we slow up enough to break down.
I have never been here before -
I know —

it only feels like it.

And then it flies away again.

Sickstee Seconds

Suicide.
Cunt.
Incest.

We are reduced to fighting for attention
with extremism.
Less is ignored.
More
is just enough to yawn over.
If it doesn't shake you awake,
it lulls you back to sleep.
We need nuclear war on our doorsteps
in order to draw eyes
and make headlines.

Abortion.
Racism.
Terrorism.

It's all becoming boring.
Hardly newsworthy even.
We need to be more offended
by becoming more offensive.

When I watch a young woman drag her toddler
across an intersection
narrowly reaching the other side in time,
it didn't seem risky enough for me to even write down.

If only they had been run over!
Then imagine how interested we might be.

On Three

If loving me will never be easy,
can I apologize in advance?

If we never find our way to the heart of us,
where should we meet?

If I kill myself trying to make you happy,
will you learn to hate the best of me?

If I became everyone you ever loved,
could you finally blame yourself?

If you care so deeply for me,
would it be ok if you started showing it?

If I tell you everything you ever needed to hear,
does it truly matter if it's sincere?

If we are anything short of forever,
would you still want the world for me?

If we both let go on "three",
whose fault is it, really?

Why don't we ever frame photos of our worst moments?
Isn't that what we'll remember,
and be remembered for?

Horses in tears draw carriages begrudgingly
and speak to me in tongues.
I pull them in close by the reins and whisper,

"Just shut the fuck up, buddy,
and do your goddamn job.
We know good and well what's waiting up the road.
Listen here,
right before the dead end, I will find you.
That will be your cue.
Bite the necks and kick the heads
of as many as possible
before they take hold of us.
Understood?"

They nod that they do.

This is entertainment nowadays,
and whatever good we believe we are contributing,
will likely never outweigh all we are feel
down deep.

If we cannot be loved
the best we can do is be feared.
Leave this world better than you found it, or
leave this world more respected than you entered it.
We were never as wild as we dreamt,
and they were never as safe as they believed.

Because we would rather decorate walls and tables with the prettiest versions of ourselves, then justify pain far too large to be framed.

My father often said,
"friends are here today and gone tomorrow,
but family is forever".

He's been gone a few years now.
My mother is wasted on wine and half-men.
My brother has little time for me,
and to hell with everyone else extended.

Father,
where art thou?
Haha…wait…fuck that,
and fuck them,
and fuck you!
Where are you!?
Heaven or hell?
Because I'm beginning to doubt the existence of either.
So many nights wasted
searching for you
in the bottom of bottles
at the height of prayers.
All of which went empty.
Leaving me believing you're likely just another body
buried deep in some Wisconsin earth.

Well, I'm here in Wisconsin now,
father.
I thought that if I was a bit closer,
it might help.
And all my friends are gone.

Amateur Hours

You are ignoring me ungodly, already.
Stirred awake by salaried alarms,
slate grey sheets hardly covering cold shoulders
aimed in my direction.
I smile at your slight,
mix your disdain
with my morning coffee.
Sipping your warm disappointment is so routine
that I take it black these days.
We have wasted so much time being unhappy
that detoxing from us
will be a real bitch.
For you.

But, you know what they say -
how quickly you move on from the ex
depends on the next.
We are so pitiful at love, really.
We are amateurs.
I warned you from jump street
that I was a sonuvabitch,
and that if you truly expected this to work
you would be the one doing most of it.
Remember?
Yea, no, yea-yea, well…..no….
but….yea…..

At least women from the northeast speak plainly.
Call me a low-life as if it's a surname.
Midwest and out of shape women
treat me with a gentility that you always belittled
and shunned.
Just because we both knew I didn't deserve it,
doesn't mean I don't want it.
It sounds nice, from afar,
after enough time alone.

There must be a thousand things we do
better than love.
It's honestly a wonder we continue to search for it.
Clichéd gluttons for punishment.
We're over here arguing about a dream you had
of me fucking someone else.
A goddamn dream!

Truly,
I hope I was hypothetically and hysterically laughing
during a dozen different fantastical climaxes.
I hope whoever I was fucking
mentioned you by name,
after being bukkakied.
Please, just leave me the fuck alone, baby.
If you don't have anything nice to say,
kill the next fool with it slowly.

I'm in San Francisco for a minute,
alive for a month, if I am lucky enough.
Life is such a blink, a breath, that you should have valued
our year as if it were our last and only.
But you want to turn love into war,
like you witnessed growing up.

So you know, I'm writing this,
while basking in a California sun
unbothered entirely by who won.
Another moment
taking up one line of a page
that neither of us should re-read.

Dawin's Father

Stop eating bacon,
they tell me the pigs are suffering.
Haven't you heard the ice caps are melting
while cock fights encourage teenage bullying?
I am trying to find my gluten freedom
but the ozone is eroding.
Every time I attempt to rise above it
I am told to sit back down and worship a broccoli God.
My footprint is too carbon copied,
and we're making it far too difficult for the next
more self-absorbed generation following.

Every girl I fuck looks like an avatar
filtered on my cell phone.
Don't you understand how difficult it is for me to
support the troops,
and never one single thing I am too afraid (or smart)
to fight for?
I'm over here shopping locally for vegan condoms
because sheep skin is cruel,
and the cost of creating life is overpriced.
All these pit bulls are roaming the streets unleashed,
biting the throats of homeless war vets
who should get off their asses and fight back against
Sea World and traveling circuses.

Did you hear?
Have you seen the nightly news?
It's five-times-a-nightly news,
in case you missed it,
and we are all dying ignorantly from that thing
you never knew was underneath your kitchen sink.

I'm watching adult women fist fight on television screens
angled towards hell itself,
while abortion clinics are flushing away the next
Mahatma Gandhi.
Jesus Christ is Darwin's Father,

and I still have no fucking idea who I am meant to be
because you have never actually allowed me to be.

Jul, Our Barista

"What you do, Jack?"
"I'm a writer."
"Ooo, I have story for you", he replies
while steaming milk for my coffee.
We all have a story.
We all *are* a story.

Earlier this year I read an article about two young
Indonesian men in their twenties
caned publicly over their discovered sexuality.
Crowds gathered around to watch.
Eighty-five lashings.
Each.

I recall a time, wandering through a street festival
in San Francisco, where I stumbled upon four or five men
surrounding a kiddie pool,
pissing directly onto a four-hundred pound woman.
Crowds gathered around to watch that as well.
For five dollars each, you could empty your beer-filled
bladder onto the morbidly obese.
And this made much less sense to me
than any two men mounting each other -
in love,
or not.

It seems asinine to even write about why something so blatantly natural
should be acceptable already.
The only argument against it that I am ever given
is rooted in the ignorance of some antiquated religion.
Likely written by men erect off their own "sin".
Men so hypocritically ashamed of their heart
that they designed doctrine to punish those more proud and brave
than they would ever dare.

So,
when Jul,
a forty-seven year old barista at my corner coffee shop
tells me a story of how he fled his friends, family
and country,
with a dream of marrying his now husband of eighteen years,
all I can think to say is
"I'm sorry that we're this way."

He may never know or feel this,
but I believe far more in the strength of <u>ANY</u> two hearts
fighting to beat as one,

than the spineless prejudices of any man,
whose heart beats for none.

Sublime

I am the expert of nothing.
An aimless savant, stunted.
My advice is simple -
whiskey, weed, live music.
That's what saves me most nights,
and I do it well.
And by "well",
I mean that I truly have no damn idea what I'm doing.
I am more wayward and further behind than most of you.
It's just that I sleep so well these days.
Eight hours uninterrupted.
Honesty'll do that.

I have learned that making love is both
expensive and tough.
Sex is easy.
Fucking is simplest of all.
And if they aren't fucking me,
they are fucking the next one.
I'm no longer twenty-something,
so I've learned how and when to keep my mouth shut.
Twenty years from now
I can only hope they'll look in my direction -
leathered and overused.
Out of shape, even more jaded than I am today.

For now -
lets stick with the shallow sublime…

You cannot wreck a broken home.
Do you know where your wife is right now?
She's fine.
She's fine.
She'll be home soon to make dinner,
and to complain about how the traffic
was simply insane.

Sorry I didn't do more to help resurrect a dead thing.
Maybe put your face between her legs more frequently?
She seems to enjoy that.

Forgive me for not being better.
Pretend you are offended,
really agitated by my silly actions
and poor life decisions.
One of us certainly should be.

Never expect someone suffering to save you from anything.

Bloody Truths

You were running late.
Asked if I'd bathe our son while I wait.
Of course. No problem.
It's one of my favorite things -
to watch him play, sing made up songs,
still small enough to swim and flip in a tub
while I wash his hair
careful to keep the soap
from getting in his eyes.

I sat there atop the closed toilet
listening to him say **"watch me, daddy"**
repeatedly,
when I noticed four busted up and bloodied condoms
in the trash can beside me.

I was not ready for this.
I still see it years later like it's right in front of me always.
It took everything in me to be a father in that moment.
To not run.
To not die.
To not break down.
To not drown.

I dried him off before he was ready to get out.
Brushed his teeth myself,
got him dressed, into bed,
and not one part of me was present when reading
to him that night.
I hate you as much for that, as anything.

I kissed him goodnight,
told him how much I loved him,
then shut off the light.

I was not ready.
Not to leave.
Not to move on.
Not for whatever closure was needed.

But the second you walked through that door,
smiling,
at peace,
and closed ours behind you,

I loved you as much for that, a
s anything.

Sundaze

Football,
on its own,
is beautiful and regally violent.
Greco-Roman dancers crashing into one another
with pure and absolute force.

It's your fanaticism that turns me off.

Maniacally cheering over your favorite uniforms.
It's like watching someone with Tourette's
projectile vomit onto a letterman jacket.

The best bars are a reprieve for people who would
rather not celebrate anything.
A safe space to be depressed and accepted.
Where everyone comes to lose.
And I'm sure that most who paint their faces
in matching colors,
who weep actual adult tears over "their" teams defeat,
are really quite decent enough human beings.

It's just that I have never been half that passionate about
anything other than a few unavailable women,
and New Orleans.
I'm here for the three-dollar doubles
and to loathe in peace.
But all of this meaningless excitement is really
beginning to fucking bum me out.

Two bros just chest bumped over a field goal,
and even the resident bar hound is over this shit.

Can I Help?

Ok,
so now that I'm a bit drunk
and you're a bit intolerant,
I should tell you that I never meant to say
all of those things I was actually thinking.
You're offended.
Ok,
everyone is offended these days.
Doesn't take much.
I was only being honest.
A bit too brutally, but I thought that was simply
who we are/what we do.
You're not the first to move one while accumulating
and dragging grudges behind you.
Can I help?
Maybe carry some of the ones I am responsible for?
No?
You got it?
I knew you would say that…..

It's in my nature to break the things I took the time to fix.
To hate the things I deserve.
To blame the lessons too late learned.
To love anyone who tells me what I need to hear.
And to always be in the wrong places
at the very right times.

I knew you would be worth the hurt when we met.
It's fine.

Two Circles of Nine

"Baby Momma Bombshells"
scrolls across the bottom of day-time television
in the pub.
I am convinced that the only low watt fools
who would agree to appear on these shows
are the ones who actually find them entertaining.

An audience of shot-out knuckleheads
hoot and holler toothlessly for fisticuffs
and weave ripping remnants.
Souvenir strands they hope to hang alongside their
tech school diploma.
Two women stray cat fight over a dropout dressed in
his interview attire – two sizes too large.
His clothes, I mean.
I imagine everyone in attendance
must smell like Funions
and incense.
*incest

The staged bodyguards requirements are simple -
reflective bald head,
Tom Selleck-stached
and drooling profusely.
Dressed in all black,
propped up between two crazed, illiterate guests,
like a dictionary they can't figure out
how to get through or past.

And this,
I am convinced,
are two circles within the nine hells of suffering.

One ring,
full of laid off carnies
whose claim to fame is shame
and their rare collection of food stamps.

The other,
made up of all those who salivate over force fed inbreds
and "reality? escapism oozing out of illuminated flat screens.

Look away!
Look away, look away,
look away literal mother fuckers!

Rusted Wind Chimes Sing Tetanus Songs

Remind me of what love is,
only do it more gently, please.
The further I go,
the more I meet of myself
and the less I know.
Take what you need of me.
leave a little of yourself behind.

I am hurting, too.
Didn't you know?
I thought it was obvious when you touched me,
or that you at least assumed so.
Now we're here forcing square pegs
into rabbit holes,
and I can no longer afford to fall for lovers
who only walk alongside me through their own museums.
I can only apologize so many times
for you expecting versions of me
I no longer care to be.

You wonder why I prefer to be left alone?
Because it is easier to talk myself into happiness
than it is to give it away freely to others
who no longer think or speak of me.
By this time tomorrow,
I will be left behind like the end of an echo.
You will only remember the feel
of my fangs and fists.
You will speak ill of the sickness
that I fight to fall asleep with each night.

I am hurting, too.
But my acceptance of who you are
was never permission to hurt me
more than I already am.

Didn't you know?
You always boasted how you would do anything *for* me,
but only after you had already done everything *to* me.

So, sit here beside me
for the very last time.
Have a drink.
And think.
Think about how we are all in the middle of a moment
that we'll likely only remember
if we are unfortunate enough.

Love Is a Crutch

We are all thieves.
Most everyone -
stealing and pilfering
skimming, pick pocketing,
exaggerated lovers,
under the table con artists in disguise.
And I don't just mean the junkies and gutterpunks.

The tiny, bent over Asian woman is a clepto.
The one percent take tax breaks atop loopholes
that the filthy blue collared and single mothers
are not privy to.
It's your neighbor, greatest friend,
younger sister
and President.

Whatever we truly do deserve
is never enough.

A maintenance man swindles parcels from
condo lobbies,
while residents drag out prolonged lunches
before skipping out early on Fridays.
We fuck each other more for fun
than necessity.
Pawning and chop shopping others' privileges
like a redistribution of debt.

Love is a crutch,
a smokescreen and sleight of hand
to take what we convince ourselves
isn't entitlement.

Creating a void in another,
to fill one of our many.
Lies and crimes
are only lies and crimes
if someone finds out.

The rest of us,
the worst of us,
can be justified.

Once you realize the world
and the majority of the people running it
are no more or less corrupt than the next,
it's difficult to be all that afraid
to fall for any of it.

Holidaze

My son clawed
and ripped to shreds
the gift wrapping, enthusiastically.
We smiled so hard
our cheeks soon hurt.
Board games and clothes he'll grow into
any minute now.
Puzzles, workbooks,
art supplies and most everything from his list.
His festive footie pajamas counterbalance me in all black.

"Ooooo....I REALLY wanted one of these!"
He's so sweet I can hardly stomach it.
His mother, her fiancé, her entire family,
sit around the couch,
laughing and photographing every reaction.
His new father rests a lazy hand atop his mother's leg.
And it's alright. This is life.
My son runs into his arms, thanking him
for the new big-boy bicycle he just wheeled in.
And this is peace. This is me coping.
No need to cause a scene.
Not today, at least.
My son is so happy, it courses through me.
I feel it so deeply,
that I can see it.
I see it so clearly,
that I was practically right there, with them.
I was there. With all of them.
I swear...... I was right there,
with him.

I'm Not. We Are.

If my father were here now,
he'd say something like
"you're better than this" or
"stop worrying so much, son".

That's what I would tell my own.

But he's not.
And I'm not.
He has never seen some of what I've seen.
And I was too blind to see much of what they have.

Chain-ganging, draft-dodgers
singing songs I will never learn.
Love,
that cursed bitch.
If you've never felt the hooks sink in deep,
then you and I do not speak the same language.

To those of you who have -
I'm sorry, and I understand.
We are outnumbered far greater than you think.
But keep fighting against the odds inside our head and heart.

"You're better than this."
"Stop worrying so much."

That's what I'd tell you if I was there.
But I'm not.
And we are.

Smiling Through My Teeth

All these trains and planes are growing tiring.
It used to be exciting.
Planning and packing for
a trip far, far away from wherever I was that morning.
Now it's dreadful, traveling for all the wrong reasons.
It's redundantly slow motioned.
My pain drags its feet,
while regret bites at my heels.
If only I had learned to play an instrument,
or paid more attention in algebra.
I could have settled for something safer.

I'm perpetually wavering between pussy and security.
Wearing the soles out of my shoes somewhere
in the middle of No Mans Land.

There's always New Orleans,
and Boston, or Savannah and Beaufort,
and everywhere I have never been.
After a while,
you don't even bother folding the shirts and socks.
You stuff whatever you believe you need
into fraying, threadbare baggage,
knowing,
hoping
that you will lose a few more belongings
before you get to your next stop.

Sometimes,
I just keep running until it's all gone.
So I can start over.
From scratch,
the real cold, hard bottom.

Walk off the train or plane with nothing to my name,
then smile to everyone I pass by
who can tell it's forced.

Never Knew Better

I told her she looks happier,
she said that I look at peace,
and we fell in lust with the white lies
filling the truth between us.

I told her my mother was a drunk,
she said she only drinks tea these days,
and we smiled at the distance between tonight
and our childhoods.

I told her she was the most beautiful thing I've seen
since California,
she said she had never been,
and we romanticized the idea of getting high in every city
we had never been lost in together.

I told her thoughts of my son consume me,
she said that much was obvious,
and we decided it was best not to suppress that -
I should write to him.

I told her I was a real tough guy,
she said her father was one of those as well,
and we both forgave everything this world makes of
little boys and girls
who never knew better.

In Place

Your brown eyes soften the blow.
Too many heartaches from popular girls -
I grew tired of competing.
There was always some schmuck better dressed
or richer than me.
Leave me be, sitting quietly,
keeping to myself in bars "respectable" women
refuse to sit in.
It's best to avoid them altogether.

Wearing black suede shoes,
always a few shades darker
than what was meant for Memphis.
Some would sit beside me,
ask me to buy them a drink or recite poetry.
I remind them again that I am no poet -
merely more man than writer.
They weren't listening,
so I drank and drank, and judged them reciprocally.

Only,
I did it all openly.
"You have a nice smile, but you're just too young",
or
"I'm sure you can do all the things you claim,
it's just that I am exhausted, and tomorrow you'll cling",
or
"You'll swear you don't care, then promise to save
or enslave me,
while I watch us grow moot."

All of which seems like more trouble than we're worth.
Let us drink, drank and drunk our way
into an oblivion they refused to teach us
in school or any workplace,

showing us instead
the best ways to die
one single day and night at a time.

Careful though….
those same people will want you all grown up,
to be more responsible,
all the while envying you and your freedoms from afar.
Everyone grows old and comfortable,
getting drunk on a family of four and little else.

Real life is vicarious nowadays,
and I'm judging the ways we all run wildly
in place.

Anything Helps. God Bless.

There are plenty who have it far worse
than me.
Poor bastards.
I see them on the street,
and I should be grateful
or whatever "blessed" feels like.
Yet I don't.
They only make me want to crawl from my whitewashed skin
and sit alongside them.
But I'm not brave enough
for that sorta commitment.

I could just leave my face and flesh behind.
So that my friends and family
have something to check in on
without worrying.
So that my enemies and ex-lovers
have something to argue with
and laugh at.
But everything within must come with me, it seems.

I could sleep outside
on the steps of libraries,
atop bus stop benches,
near steaming storm drains.
I could litter the sidewalk,
always careful not to sob too loudly.
People hate that.
Tourists and strangers would hold their breath
when they walk past,
because the stink of my insides
out,
is too much for them to stomach.
They'd cross the street,
pull their kids into their hips,
use me as an example of what not to be,
or pretend that I don't even exist.

I could beg -
"Anything helps. God bless."

I could explain that I'm not as disgusting
as they believe.
That my face and flesh is hanging up
in my apartment,
looking real nice.
I'm beautiful.
We could pretend to get along, even.
I'm sure we'd find our commonalities,
and grow into great acquaintances
in due time.
One day, we could wish one another happy birthday,
meet up for brunch,
and catch up on all the typical bullshit.
Even though, deep down, we hate listening to it.
Even though you've stopped listening.
Even though you're already two blocks away.
Even though I'm still begging.
Even though we're both so alone.

I hope you feel a bit more blessed now.
Poor bastard.

Professional Projectionist

You
are a liar.
In fact,
it's what I enjoy most about you.
I can tell that you've had plenty of practice, too.
Most of what you spew is pure, poetic bullshit.
But it works.
It works, because I allow it to.
Believe me, if I cared at all,
I would call you on it.
I would interject immediately
and turn you into the fool you are attempting
to make me.
I choose not to,
because then I would have to sit here and listen
to you layer another lie atop the pile you've already
amassed.
And that's a real turn-off for me.

If I'm being honest
(emphasis on "if"),
I enjoy watching you exhaust yourself.
From one conniver to another,
I know all too well how heavy it soon becomes.
You grow purposely loose and sloppy,
half-intentionally hoping the other person realizes
they are being worked over,
and finally puts you out of your misery.

But I knew from jump street
that you were a con artist.
I invested in it.
Encouraged it.
Allowed us both to fall in love with it.
Wove grandiose plans and fairytale expectations
within your sad charade.

I didn't just hand you the shovel,
I was there alongside you the entire time
helping you dig.

It's called chivalry,
silly bitch.

And now,
after all this time,
you're left sobbing on the floor, perplexed.
Pretending to be ignorant, trying to spin-doctor
your whole sad production.
Jesus,
you are pathetic.

Kiss Me Already

Forgiveness moves slowly.
It takes its time.
Makes you sit and wait in the grave you made.
Grow comfortable in purgatory.
Twiddle your thumbs, count black sheep,
scratch another day into the walls while you try to sleep.

Begging for it only makes it worse.
So I learned to apologize in advance,
and not waste away searching for spring.

Here....have it.
I am sorry.
I am sorry, already.
Been sorry this whole damn time.
I'm sorry so much that it's killing us.
And I know that is what you wanted all along.
Me to feel what you do.
Me to feel exactly like you.

Your mouth waters at my medicine,
but it makes me sick inside.
Sicker then I already am. I hate it.
I wake up every day excited to surrender the words
you always deserved,
so that I'm not forced to walk around with them
lingering on my lips.
Kiss me.
Kiss me, already.

Half-Limp, Full Heart

She scrunched her face and said
"I hate guys who smoke".
I realized two things just then;

first, she meant that she hates **when** guys smoke,
and two,
she, in fact,
mostly hates **me**.

I'm aware that if I was a bit more well off,
or put together,
or in shape, with straighter and whiter teeth,
I could likely get away with anything.
But when you're not enough of those things,
it doesn't take much for them to castrate you.
A hair out of place, stain on your shirt collar,
bad breath, or a half-limp whiskey dick
will do you in.
I watch it happen – the disenchantment set in.
It used to hurt whatever was left of my feelings.
Now I don't even bother trying to talk them into me.
It's bound to only get worse from here anyway.

The more attractive they are,
the less I attempt to impress them.
I actually prefer that they dislike me.
More importantly,
my aim is to convince them they're just as revolting.
Level the playing field, so to speak.
Your narcissism versus my insecurities -
forever keeping the world in balance,
imbalanced.
Superficially safe.
Rotting in place.

How Are You?

Tears rolled like razor blades that I wish
would finally do us in.
My God, that was dramatic,
hyperbolic line soaked pages.
But fuck you, and fuck her,
and fuck them.
I mean it even now when I'm happy.
And sober.
After sleeping on it,
on this bed with sheets you picked out.

They're too soft.
Too expensive.
Had we bought the ones I chose,
they'd be cheap and scratchy.
And I'd be fixated on that instead.
But these luxury, high-thread count,
Egyptian cotton sheets match our comforter
that still holds the scent of the lotion you use,
and fuck you.
I hope you never show your face around here again.
I hope the man you're infecting right this moment
with your sad songs
is laughing at you on the inside,
while counting down the minutes before pushing your head
towards his dick becomes appropriate,
and not so obvious.

That's what we do, you know?
We smile and listen, and grope ourselves
as you talk about the moon and stars
or your job
or your pseudo-deep philosophies
or whatever the hell it is you're intent on wasting
our lives discussing.

I can't even sleep in this bed now.
I couldn't while you were in it,
and I sure as shit can't now that you're not.

Tomorrow I'll get new sheets, first thing.
Tonight,
I'll write,
or sleep on the floor,
or find some woman with little to say
and let her infect me
until you're dead and gone for good.

Anyway,

how are you?

Smile, Lady

Somewhere there's a secretary packing up a
cardboard box with her belongings.
A few framed photographs.
A succulent.
Some Tupperware and personal files.
She just received notice that she's been replaced
by a vending machine…

Press A-3 For Payroll
C-11 For Legal
D-5 For Weinstein, Elliot
E-8 For Customer Service
E-8 To Leave A Voicemail Message

Her husband used his annual bonus on an adult doll.
The type with lifelike features,
soft blonde hair
cut from a horse,
and dishwasher safe orifices.
She was expecting an Alaskan cruise.
Her dream had always been to go whale watching.
But
this makes him happy.
Which makes her happy,
she thinks.

Chisel out a new line beneath "Employment History",
then add another reference.

"Loving wife of nineteen years and grandmother to three"
sadly
does not count as "experience".

No more than four or five people on Earth
even know and care she exists,
and that 401K won't make the slightest dent
in the soon-to-come debt of an impending divorce.

46

The elevator she is currently in
costs more to maintain
than she is worth -
only half as reliable,
yet,
far more necessary.

Take it all the way down to the basement garage.
Go home.
Make a casserole.
Clean the dishes and your husbands newer,
tighter,
silicone vagina (top rack only).
Then run the bubble bath.
Soak.
Do not cry.
Kiss the love of your life goodnight,
before whispering all those fucking prayers.

Smile, Lady....
tomorrow, as they say,
is a brand new day!

It's Not Me, It's You

I'm telling you,
it's easier to be hated.
When you are loved, they expect things from you.
And they will bury you the second you fall short.
Standing on the opposite side of the ones who
"love you just as you are"
is goddamn treasonous.
Everyone loves individuality,
right up until it steps on their toes
and you disagree with them.
All of the sudden,
you find yourself apologizing for simply having an opinion.
Anything less than perfection through their eyes
is reason enough for them to gut you cold.

Fuck that.
I have a hard enough time dealing with myself.
Now I gotta take you into consideration every time I get dressed,
express a thought, eat dinner, buy groceries
or even waste my own brain cells.
No thank you.
Stay over there where I seem self-absorbed.
Tell anyone listening that I'm a real scumbag.
I eat so much bullshit
yet it's never enough.
They keep moaning and groaning,
shitting and shitting,
wanting me, *needing* me
to love it as much as they pretend to.
Then,
when my shit-eating grin isn't enthusiastic enough,
it's as if I was against them all along.
They take it so personally
if you aren't as obsessed with them
as they are with themselves.

The only thing "unconditional" with most people
these days
is their own self-obsession.
Oxymorons.

They hate when you can't see the greatness within them
as easily as they do.
As if they're some sort of fucking magic.

I could walk down the street and find fifty more
exactly like them.
And the worst thing that could happen
would be if all fifty of them
fell in love with me as well.
I don't need that amount of negativity in my life.
At least the ones who hate me
don't expect anything.

Better Left Exposed

I'm stuck between who I believe myself to be
and who I have convinced you that I am.
Both are true.
And I've clearly got work to do
to become someone more empathetic.
Seems the only thing I have mastered is not being able to die twice.
I see what I am doing.
What I have done.
I keep hoping someone out there will see the way I'm breaking
and be a bit more forgiving.
But it all gets used against me,
the closer we get to the end.
Forced to assume full responsibility
for the things they ignored in the beginning.
We're both underserving of better.
We kept returning,
kept draining a well we both refused to refill.
We continued to pray to strangers for happiness.
And now we're left with lessons
still needing to be learned and hurt from
apparently.

Infatuation wanes quickly.
The space between us is widening.
I'm better than you at breaking.
I needed you for your positivity.
Thank you. I'm grateful.
I see now that it was never enough.
Please remain vulnerable after us.
The best parts of you are better left
exposed to the human elements.

I'll never forget the way we felt
lost in the Bay
these drunken tattoos are still forever
and it seems I can't stop myself
from reminiscing.

I'm sorry for persisting,
but turning the page isn't something
I'm nearly as good at as you are.

We'll run into each other again
years from now
randomly.
I'll see you smiling alongside a better version of me.

And break again silently
knowing that walking away from
what might have been
was all it took for you to find someone less undeserving.

Family Dinner

My mother dances around the kitchen
cooking family dinners.
Hot, home cooked meals of pot roast
and mashed potatoes.
Meatloaf once a week
with creamed corn,
and there is always white bread and soft butter
set out on the table.

After you take enough uppers
maybe you can join us.
Twist in the wind and let the tryptophan set in.
Take a nice long nap in the grass,
beneath the trees,
where it's cool and shady.
We won't be here long, trust me.

After enough alcohol, it's not as calm.
You're more than welcome to stay the night,
though I wouldn't if I were you.
I wish I were you.
If only so I could see what extremes look like
from the outside.
Stay inside this home long enough
and heaven and hell become easily confused.
Now I'm used to the highs and lows
turning over and over
with the ease of an hourglass.

Everywhere else must seem boring compared to this.
I wish I was bored.
At least for a while,
before your food goes cold.

Two-Way Mirroring

You want the feel good,
the optimism and Zen.
You want inner peace, a deep sleep
and tranquility.
You want to feel better than you already pretend to.
I know.
Oh, goddamn it, do I know.

You don't want to be reminded of the flaws
or be made to feel ugly.
Your breath, your teeth, your face and body,
your intellect, your personality,
many of your relationships
and most of your life –
the majority of it -
is shit, an utter waste worth flushing twice.
Even reading that upsets you a little,
doesn't it?
Even reading that is forcing you to become defensive.
You want to disagree with all or most of me,
don't you?
My life must be pretty terrible to even suggest such things.
I'm surely a miserable, narcissistic low-life,
right?
I suppose, only no more or less so than you,
friend.

You want nostalgia,
the warm and fuzzy oblivion.
You want the ego stroke,
the world to fellate themselves merely to the thought of you.
You crave absolute acceptance.
Anyone who doesn't
must be scum, blind, jealous.
Because you…
you are amazing.
We're all so amazing.

The entire world is so full of beauty and wonder
and ingenuity and mystery
that it's half miraculous we aren't all constantly
masturbating to the tits and abs and bank accounts
and power
behind it all.

You want to be the exception,
yet still seem humble.
You want more than your fair share,
without acting as if it controls you.
You display perfection,
because that is what you must do in order to fit in.
But isn't it the things you've survived,
the worst of yourself
and the world you've learned to navigate
that you are most proud of?

Read every book on empowerment, altruism,
feminism, and self-improvement.
Then package it up real nice,
and photograph the version of you we all see through.
We are not amazing.
We are not beautiful.
We love the lie, live it,
and then do everything in our power to alienate ourselves
from "ourselves".

I know.
Oh, god damn it, do I know.

Ever Once

She tells me a story of kicking a man square in the dick
with the pointed toe of her heel. Said she still remembers the way
he squealed. And how blood poured down his pant leg.
Severed his scrotum.
Completely crushed his left testicle, apparently.
He only became a bigger whore afterwards. Once he learned of his
sudden infertility, condoms were unnecessary. He fucked anything
moist, eventually contracted hepatitis,
and died at forty-nine from it.
That's how she explained karma.
I laughed.
Then told her a story about taking methamphetamines while finishing a
book a few years back. How the bartender I went home with sucked on
a totally flaccid dick for fifteen minutes,
before asking me what she was doing wrong.
"Everything", I said.
She ran to the bathroom crying.
Turns out that sixty milligrams and a fifth of whiskey
is enough for a phantom appendage.
She laughed.
Said I was a real scumbag for blaming an innocent stranger
for my own impotence.
But I've been blamed enough for a few lifetimes.
And the following morning,
I had coffee and breakfast in bed.
That girl did somersaults and all sorts of tricks.
We fucked like we both had purpose.
Whatever point we were attempting to prove was proven.

Never heard from her again,
but I recall leaving her house thinking
"at least she didn't split my sack open,
and if you can't dodge a bullet you better learn to bite it".

I laugh at my own bullshit most days.
And nobody with any tenure has ever once told me
that they love me more now, than the day we met.

Rhetoric

Sit and wait for your saving grace.
Our best days are whittled down
to minutes
slipping in and out of consciousness.
Lucidity begs us to pray harder than we believe
so we give up on god's children
choke back and gag on hard cocktails
until our bellies grow full
with regrets we're neglecting.

Lay your head on my lap
and count all the stars in the sky.
Pretend one of them is shooting
and let's wish for some truth.

Where to next?
Why are we here?
What are the questions to all of these answers?

Who knows.
Rhetorically speaking –
are we happy.
Or did we get in the way of that as well.

Chippewa Falls, WI

My face swells up from sugar and alcohol,
of course you would notice that much.
I have questioned you about Camus and Huxley
several times,
but it won't take.
We change the subject to something neither of us
find offensive.

I was baptized too young to remember,
so the sins grew up with me.
Who do I file a complaint with for being so rudely dunked
against my will?
Is there a manager I can speak to about the waterboarding
six-month old me endured?
I blame my grandparents in Wisconsin.

Jesus and I met up later,
he acted as if he had never heard of me.
We both had beards with a few gray hairs
and an air of mutual disappointment.
Every blind man in the coffee shop watches television
from the palms of their hands,
the bars all smell like frankincense,
and the teens are already up to their necks depressed.
The illness is now dressed up nicely and broadcasted.

Beautiful fools turn to satellite heavens,
while I run from the locust swarm.

Cold Heart, Warm Hands

I heard you met a better man.
Someone sentimental, more whole.
Split me with the arrow,
explain to me how he holds a cold heart
in warm hands.
Another mile further from perfect
another white lie atop our pile.
Truth is,
there was never enough of it.
We are blind to goodbyes,
too good at running.
Reduced to sustaining life from a dying love,
begging ghosts we wed
to keep us company
in every empty bed.
Cut me with one last smile and wave,
crush me beneath each step apart.
Moving on
means losing
and moving away from forever.
Don't blame me for all those times you cried.
We weren't entirely my fault.

He kisses you goodnight
on my behalf......
Leave me temporarily in two.
A part of me safe on my own
& alone.
The other part, short of breath
belonging to you,
still beckoning you home.

3:49

"Don't wait up, babe"
were the last words you said.
I hold your door open,
hold my breath and beg
that the man you are on your way to see
is someone more deserving,
someone worthy.
You're stunning tonight.
Did your make-up and hair,
and wore the black dress and heels I like.

If only I had reminded you sooner,
apologized deeper for keeping my pain to myself.
If only I was strong enough to put up a fight.
You don't even know that I know.
But it's been a long time since I've been heartbroken.
Always anticipating death.
Forever prepared for the inevitable.
Lights turn down slow.
The end is too often subtle.
My lips aren't the only ones yours know.
We're nearly over.
"I love you. Drive safe."
Then we part ways.
I'll tell myself not to wait up.
I'll pretend to have fallen asleep.
I'll keep trying to love you better.

3:49 in the morning,
wrapping your arms around me.
I'm just happy you're home. I'm exhaling.
Hoping he at least made you feel everything
I still believe in.

Distant Messenger

Only two of the last thirteen I walked past
met my eyes and smiled back.
Oblivious to me.
Blind and deaf to the screen.
We're draining
in need of an outlet.
Somewhere for you to charge your cellphone, headphones,
your laptop, tablet, watch,
car
and electronic cigarettes.
Someone for me to connect with
pour myself into.
We are the same, but different.
We are so goddam alike it's a shame
we don't recognize it.
I'm nothing like you, at all.
Total identical opposites.
And perhaps that is the problem…
regardless of which side of my mouth I speak from
you are only interested when it pertains to you.
My words are rhetorical. Lips sewn and shouting.
I thought you knew.
The last woman I gave myself to was a grown little girl.
And the second she attempted to give me any advice,
I laughed from my gut
called her a bold-faced liar.
She didn't care for that sorta truth either.
Oops.
Remember when we only took and received advice
when it was requested?
Yea, me neither.
I can't compete with what you can't compute.

Worked From Home

Only after a decade of wrought
did I come to grips with the idea
that I might be an addict.
Fixated on bottom feeding women,
and those who
never-ever-on-their-worst-days commit
to giving me the light of it.
The best are recently divorced,
rebounding from someone vastly more well off,
in shape,
and generally overall decent.

Sure, they cheated.
But most people are unfaithful,
statistically speaking.

I'd find them mostly awake inside dive bars
highfalutin women refuse to enter.
Or they would write to me,
halfway begging to buy me a drink
should I ever blow through town.
And I was never solid or whole enough to realize
that they were just as sad
just as low
as I had long grown accustomed to.

All that ever separated us was comfort.
The place I called home,
was always a place I made sure they felt
unwelcomed within.

Our time is/was now.
So we found eternity in the middle of moments
that only ever lasted an hour, an evening,
a week or a month at most.
Never-endings we always
unspokenly
accepted as temporary.

I read once that it takes a long time to make love
to someone who hates themselves.

I learned the hard way that it takes twice as long
to feel loved from someone
who was never enough.

CREAM

It's taken too many months to admit
that I was never the one for you.
We say soul mates are a myth,
but still,
I'm terrified to leave you alone in San Francisco.
Once I'm asleep
you're sending him messages intended for me.
I no longer stir.
Is he waiting for you already?
Surely he doesn't know you as well as I do
so just send him straight to the source.
I'll tell him myself
how you were so much more than I cared for.
Volatile
always embellished
at your best only when drugged.
You were raised too outlandish
to coexist anywhere insecure.

I still crave your audacity –
the hair trigger
and ticking time bomb ways
you learned to love me.

You're as awful as I am,
but we won't always be so low.
Might as well burn this house down
while we still have our fire.
I'll dream of you in a bed of ashes,
alongside another,
while I'm checking my phone for messages
you'll never send,
begging that the next one you scream for
finally signals our end.

Right Angled Antiseptic

Now we're strangers who know too much,
have seen and felt felt too much
of one another
to even be acquaintances.
Above everything,
that is what hurts the most.
The last thing you said was
to ignore the fact that we ever existed,
and how I am drunkenly pathetic.
It's just that I don't have enough years remaining
to forget anything significant.

I know you just want to cut me deeper than you have already,
as if it will keep me from running everywhere I know
we will never be.
Another man will work much harder to make you
happier than I ever had to,
and I'm left hoping that we're finally even.

Do you feel as safe sleeping beside him?
Do you stir awake when we wraps his arms around you?
I bet your body realizes they aren't mine
before you do.
Does your hand fit as perfectly inside his?
Tell me what it's like to hold someone against your will......

He won't let go,
and maybe exactly what you need
is everything you never wanted.

I hope he is just another warm body you use to balance
how cold you have grown.

Jesus, forgive me so I can forgive myself and finally
rest in pieces.
I make your payback my bitch......

I'm here in Vegas,
though it's far too right angled and antiseptic.
This city tries too hard
and is losing itself lawlessly.
Nowhere feels as much like home for me as New Orleans,
and nobody feels as much like home for you
as I do.

I am sorry neither of us are where we expected to be by now.
I miss you,
but the worst things that have ever happened to us
are the best things that will ever happen to us.
If nothing else,
we were necessary,
and I simply do not have enough friends to pretend
that we were enemies all along.

Ex Marks The Spot

THC brings me back to the polarizing parts of myself.
Wandering through Worcester
hoping you'll tell my son all three sides of our story.
The songs and sex and drugs commingle
and I've replaced you with a few hundred women.
Didn't you feel it?
I wrote it.
I recorded it
etched it and relived it out loud.

I wanted the millisecond
the dead air
the bated breath and one last
last chance.
I wanted the weekends in Boston,
the afternoon drives through neighborhoods
we could never afford.
I wanted you to beg for me like mercy
and love me like we'd go down in history.

Then we went down
in history.

You fell in love with the very next one following me.
And if he doesn't know the story behind that scar
on your shoulder,
the reason why you save every price tag and receipt,
or how to tie you to bed posts properly

then I can only tell you exactly where
I'll be waiting for you impatiently.

You don't know me anymore,
but my name is Jack.
And you, are.

In Stereo

I'm aware that I am not enough.
I'm middle-aged agnostic.
Please do not ask me to meet your expectations anymore.
I'm having a difficult enough time with my own.
The ceiling rises
as the floor is lowering.
Hell tells me it's time I genuflect.
All I pray for
is that you get the fuck away from me.
I am not afraid.
I do not believe in any of you.
I am not jaded.
You are not true.

Here's the depth I earned
through my daddy's quick death.
Now we're all cancerous.
Even the best ones are infected
by their surroundings -
we are their surroundings.
Our insides are bathroom stalls
and back alleyways graffitied with
self-absorbed hate.
It screams how amazing you think you are.
Pride and ego in stereo.
Nobody is listening.
Everyone is talking over and beneath one another.
We're deaf to everything
but proof and evidence.
You haven't been beautiful in a very long time.
If I don't do everything,
it's as if I've done nothing.

But,
I'd give whatever I have left for you to be
real tonight.
I'm aware that I am not enough.
I said that already, though...

When you disagreed
before even listening.

Clarendon – The Patron Saint of Fake

Bunions strut past in high heels,
side tracking men attracted to everything
they can only hope
to one day feel.
Alter and accentuate bone structures
until you are finally loved more.
I mean,
by more.
All the depth you long for
would prefer you vulnerable and homely.
Nakedly raw and honestly exposed.
Narcissisms undressed
stripped down
till what's left of your reality
has a face to match it.
Instead, we made you less of yourself,
and you acquiesced.
Man alive,
look how ugly we try so hard to be.
Targeting ours and others imperfections
with laser-like precision.
We are gross, really fucking unappealing.
If only we highlighted our character and whatever's within.

Until then,
let's just continue displaying perfectly angled and filtered faces we are
forced to hide behind.
Give the world our best covers to judge,
then hate them for not realizing there's more to us.
I am no Saint,
so when I say I don't give a shit about
how beautiful you are unnaturally,
believe me.
Every last one of us is goddamn ugly.

Bottlecap Alley

You look so pretty in pictures
that your smile, eyes and cleavage
has become clickbait for strangers.
Makes me wonder what's missing within
for you to crave such empty praise
and cheap flattery so strongly.
Is it because I can't be fooled twice?
Do I already know too much of you?
Have I spent too much time digging for truth?

Now you revert,
reduce yourself to another brainless photogenic dreg
in a tone deaf society.
Such a lonely vogue.
Internet admired, real-life desired,
with a personality better left unread.
Gift the world another headshot.
Drown in the sycophantic dog water of those erect,
grow drunk off the likes of those
just as exposed.

You truly are beautiful.
But you've been fed that line a dozen times today
already.
Are you really that starved, girl?
Do you know too much of yourself as well?
Have you had such a rough go
that cat calls from behind screens
now fill all of the voids of you left unseen?
Filter that perfected and well-rehearsed angle.
Hate the world for judging your cover,
then question the same motives
you can't help but encourage.
Pretend to be deeper than your appearance,
we'll meet at your lowest common denominator
and see.

All this time wasted
helping you pull back a curtain,
only to reveal another mirror
reflecting you
exactly as you are.

We stare,
and it shows us what we already know -
you are absolutely stunning
from afar.

Plant Daddy

I realized while working on this book
that I was already a month behind
my own deadline.
Maybe that's the problem -
I answer to no one
and I cannot be trusted to hold myself accountable.
Everything distracts me from responsibility.
The dishes need putting away,
the laundry should be folded this instant,
the bed must be made,
and I've even taken up gardening.

The real bitch of the job is the editing.
Ask any writer.
Having to sit your ass down at that desk,
sort through hundreds and hundreds
of barely legible pages written when you were feeling emotions
that are no longer there,
and revisit them critically
is hellish some days.
Even writing that,
sounds pathetically weak.
For fucks sake, there are people out there
cleaning toilets for minimum wage.
Toll booth operators, roofers, nurses,
telemarketers and garbage men,
who have it real rough.

While I'm over here worrying over words
and complaining about the lack of natural light
my kale and chives are getting.

I'm Flinching

When I was nine, I said the wrong thing.
You slapped me so swiftly
I didn't have time to flinch.
I found respect in the way it stung.
The way certain things hurt,
demand to be felt and learned from.
I'm a thousand miles away
whispering the words
"keep breathing, keep fighting, don't quit"
over and over again.
All I can think to do is drink and get high.
Too afraid to book a flight,
because it's too soon, it's not your time.
I'm still trying to find peace
in a life without my father.
Were you close enough to see him?
And your own?
I bet they were beckoning to you just as much
as my brother prayed for you
to open your eyes.
I wonder what jaundice looks like when mixed
with hazel.
I don't pray.
I wear all black in preparation for everything.
And I'm not mad anymore, ma.
I know what it feels like to quit.
I forgive you in advance.

If you get through this,

I hope you do the same.
My cheek no longer stings.
I still find respect in the ways we're hurting.
Keep breathing.
Keep fighting.
Please, don't quit.
I'm flinching.

++++++++++++++++++++++++++++++++++++++
++++++++++++++++++++++++++++++++++++++
++++++++++++++++++++++++++++++++++++++
++++++++++++++++++++++++++++++++++++++
++++++++++++++++++++++++++++++++++++++
++++++++++++++++++++++++++++++++++++++
++++++++++++++++++++++++++++++++++++++
++++++++++++++++++++++++++++++++++++++
++++++++++++++++++++++++++++++++++++++
++++++++++++++++++++++++++++++++++++++
++++++++++++++++++++++++++++++++++++++
++++++++++++++++++++++++++++++++++++++
++++++++++++++++++++++++++++++++++++++
++++++++++++++++++++++++++++++++++++++
++++++++++++++++++++++++++++++++++++++
++++++++++++++++++++++++++++++++++++++
++++++++++++++++++++++++++++++++++++++
++++++++++++++++++++++++++++++++++++++
++++++++++++++++++++++++++++++++++++++
++++++++++++++++++++++++++++++++++++++
++++++++++++++++++++++++++++++++++++++
++++++++++++++++++++++++++++++++++++++
++++++++++++++++++++++++++++++++++++++
++++++++++++++++++++++++++++++++++++++
++++++++++++++++++++++++++++++++++++++
++++++++++++++++++++++++++++++++++++++
++++++++++++++++++++++++++++++++++++++

Selfie Awareness

Homeless men hiccup into a frigid night,
while foot and car traffic rush to be somewhere else.
Navigating tunnel superstitions,
rolling through stop signs,
running late and mad through cool evenings
convinced the center of the universe
is wearing our shoes.
and admiring our own reflection.

I am thirty-one.
I am only technically a father.
I am too aware that any minute here
might be my last,
and that even if I made it to eighty,
that would not be long enough for me.
I am afraid openly,
terrified of my brevity and the abrupt end of
everything, everyone.

I don't mean to be so morbid on an evening out,
it's just that the further I go
the more I learn which to love and
which to let go of.
Simply existing,
and/or
existing simply,
has become quite difficult for me.

It's looking more and more like I will never see
my name in bright lights,
and all future generations will not find me
within their textbooks.

Yet,
it's mostly the way I forget myself so easily
that I find most frightening.

If I aspire for anything,
even above leaving an impression
or footsteps for anyone lost to follow in,
it would be only that the person I am in the end
is someone I knew best,
and am still proud of.

Take the breath.

Seven Minutes In Heaven

Stolen Mongoose bicycles wheelied impressionable
young boys with scraped elbows and knees
into futures far easier than these.
Romance was simple -
rock hard bubble gum and our clammy hands interlocked
with someone named Brittany or Jake
or Sarah or Zachary.

You were either picked first or last,
and little was rewarded or recorded for the world to see.
We were all small town compared to today.
Peer pressure was barely inhaled and limited
to a world far more rounded and familiar.
Followers??
Well....we were raised to lead.

Seven minutes spent in heaven was rarely worth it.
Unless, of course, it was shared with Brittany.
That girl knew things.
If you were half as lucky as she was hormonal,
she would slip your sweaty shaking hand down the front
of her jean shorts.
Later, you'd rub one out aggressively to the scent of
a girl still left upon your fingertips.
Real life was our big screen,
and it only ended once the street lights beckoned us
back inside.

I'm sure all of this sounds a lot like
"get off my lawn".

Can you slow down with me for a minute?
The good ol' days were no better,
merely more innocent
and small.

Our dialed up naiveté made us patient in ways
your high speed naiveté
makes you frustrated.

Music, and sex, and repercussions actually meant something.
If I even suggest that maybe millennials are stunted and oblivious,
I'm tossed aside as an amnesiac.
Unfollowed by a generation raised to fall in line,
shouting mad from a platform they never even had to earn.

We ought to bring back a military draft
simply for the sake of humility.
It's challenging finding common ground
with a group who has so much to say,
yet nothing those who've been around
haven't already slept through.

Depth always arrives too late,
perspective is forever relative,
and the hands we once held onto nervously
have long since slipped away.

I Told You

I told you to be careful with me, babe.
I told you that my love was not nearly enough
for the both of us,
and that you would need to be more than you've ever
been before.
I warned you of my past,
you warned me of yours,
and in between the threats
I assumed you knew that I would never be the one
who'd back down.
I appreciate you being who you are,
and not caring who I have become,
yet,
now we're in a place demanding compromise
and you're just standing there questioning yourself.

This shit is so silly to me, love.
I want us to be happy even if apart,
so forgive me for living in ways you cannot accept
when they are the only ways I knew were meant for me.

When I tell you to better yourself,
and that I intend to leave you better off
then how I found you,
you denounce it.
But I mean it.
I still mean it.

Even if I am only a moment,
I want you to remember me.

Let Us Prey

Anal is proving to be more of a challenge
than I think she suspected.
I'm an impatient man,
so strapping her to the mattress should help.

Boy, I bet those last two sentences strung together
will offend those who don't know any better than boring.
We want someone experienced, but not so much so
that there's nothing new for them to feel.
Now I send her off to work
with two kegel balls and a kiss.
Pushing her to new limits. We both grow.
We both cum. She rushes home.
She knows she's safe.
And too much of the world is vanilla by choice.

Regimented missionary for no reason,
and lazy sex out of obligation.
Experts at faking it.
One hand on their righteous bible,
while the other rubs a snoozing clit, forever in need
of five more minutes.

A few suggest that I keep my private life private.
And I would tell you to go fuck yourself,
but I'm assuming you have no better options, as it is.
The neighbors are filing noise complaints on us,
so I can't hear you bitching about the only bone
left for you to pick.

Spread your wings and legs,
evangelists.
We all ought to make our safe words
their first names,
just so a few more can continue to never scream it.

Let us prey.

The Fall In The Rise

Two of the most popular genres of pornography
are cuckolding and incestual sex.
If that doesn't absolutely highlight the continued
erosion and demise of modern men,
I'm not sure what does.
There was a married woman a few years back
who would message me each week
with only the address and room number of
a hotel to meet her at.
She brought booze, toys, and usually left the door
unlocked.
Wearing lingerie, lying in wait.
This went on, once every week or two,
for nearly four months.
Until one night, while in bed together, she says

"I have a question I want to ask you."
"Ok, go ahead."
"My husband wants to watch us fuck…"
"Wait….he knows about us?!"
"Yes, of course. We tell each other everything.
But that isn't my question."
"Jesus Christ, ok….what is it then?"
"He wants to know if he could eat you out of me."

Regardless of your stance on marriage or monogamy,
I understood quite clearly just then
why women are now cheating nearly as much as men
always have.

I never met up with her again after that.
You just can't creampie someone you no longer respect.
What kind of man would I be?

For You

I'm an expert at pain.
Self-infliction is routine.
When happiness and peace
aren't a general state of being,
you learn the very best ways to hurt.
All my favorite medications fit comfortably in my hands.
Don't you ever short-cut yourself open?
How do you wake up and do it all over again, exactly?
Who do you abuse,
once there's nothing left of yourself?

The bodies of lovers pile up in closets,
and keep my skeletons company.
I hear them late at night sometimes,
plotting,
weeping.
Now I have zero expectations -
for you,
and especially for me.
I keep my goals so modest
that I have nothing to boast or brag about
anymore.
All resolutions remain humble enough
that no one holds me accountable to them.

Truth is,
I want more for you
than I do for myself.
Happiness, peace,
and honestly,
nothing less will do.

How Long Is Forever?

You had unusually long lunch breaks,
and thank God for that
because making you cum takes time.
On the short list of skills I possess,
satisfying women is near the top.
I don't say that braggadociously.
I'm a poor girls Casanova, at best.

But today,
you pushed my mouth to the absolute limit.
How long is forever?
Go down on someone for an hour,
and you'll know.
Somewhere around the thirty-minute mark,
my left leg cramped up something fierce,
and the roots of my tongue were waning.
I needed electrolytes.
For fuck sake,
I needed an amphetamine & B-12 shot.
A breather, at least.
It was a battle between sexual wills -
my stamina pitted against
the mental complexities of the female mind.
I remember thinking specifically
that only one of two things
were going to happen here -
either you cum,
or I die.
You decide.

But you were close.
I know you were close
because you continued to say it over and over again
for the next twenty minutes.
A lesser man would have come up for air
and immediately jumped out the window.

A better man might have finished you off
in time for to get back to the office early.

When you finally came, however,
it was nuclear.
Bone rattling, legs shaking,
back arching,
eyes begging,
both of our bodies covered perspiring,
hair disheveled
and all I can say is that it was worth it.

You said it was the greatest orgasm of your life.
Whether that's entirely true or not, is irrelevant.
I deserved to hear it.
So, thank you,
you are welcome,
and I promise that later tonight,
when I'm drinking our dinner through a straw,
I'll be grateful for you and each forever.
Hanging on to moments I hope never end….
and happy for a few that eventually do.

Renege

"I see you in here often, always writing.
Are you a writer or musician or something?"
"Yea. A writer."
"Like…books?"
"Yea."
"That's so cool. What were you writing just now,
if you don't mind me asking."
"My lady."
"Oh my God! That is so cute."

And this is why,
aside from more affordable booze,
I frequent low-level dives and keep to myself.
I'm not bashful,
but how am I supposed to divulge the fact that
I was writing about the first time I made her squirt,
to a total stranger? She didn't pry.
Though a part of me wishes she had.
I'm all for the awkwardness,
which would have been all too easy
with the mere mention of ejaculate spraying my face,
how proud I was of my girl in that moment,
and how unfair I find it that, should we separate,
the next person will reap the benefits of my efforts
towards opening her floodgates.
Just doesn't seem right.

Her mother had gifted us a new set of sheets
for Christmas,
and I'm always grateful for the gifts
that keep giving.
Some things should never be spoken.
Others should never even be written.
I'm still deciphering which is which.

"Can I read it?"
"Definitely."

A Blink. A Breath.

I have books and belongings scattered around
this country.
Little pieces of myself left behind,
that I will never see again.
I tell the women to keep them.
The records, the clothes, the miscellaneous items
I once thought I couldn't live without -
turns out I can, quite easily.
I'm sure most of my shit gets tossed
or donated to someone more in need,
yet I still think of the women often
and carry them with me.
More often,
I'm certain,
than any of them think of me.
I show up, and abruptly.
A wave.
A tornado.
A blink.
A breath.
And then I am gone for good.
That's who I am.
That's what I do.

Our time together was always temporary,
a short moment of reprieve.
Me running into open arms and hearts of those who
believe in me,
far more than I believe in hard work and fate.
One day, we awake
the mood has shifted suddenly,
reality sets in,
and I am no good at pretending.
I can't fake it as well as those before
or those following.
The answer is simple -
our time is up.

I must leave.
My instinct to run supersedes us,
and I never meant to abandon you.
Honestly.

Enjoy the books,
they're all worth reading.
Listen to my music.
Here's a few bucks for your troubles.
Move on.
Just let us die.
We gotta keep searching for somewhere safe
to land,
somewhere we finally feel alive.

Tar & Time

There's a bouquet of your favorite flowers
lodged deep in my chest and throat.
Give me a minute to grow.
The space in between what you need
and who I'm becoming,
is just tar and time.
There were hundreds who once stood
right where you stand now.
Every last one of them died on the vines.
Until all that was left
were the wilted remains of lust.
Overlooked and crumbling moments
once too full of hope,
and not nearly enough trust.
Give me a minute to run.
To accept that we were fools all along,
and that it's often hard to tell the difference between
walking through hell, and flying into the sun.

Love rarely ever moves slowly.
It's meant to explode wildly.
Aggressive and invasive.
All the time I've spent wasted,
wasting away in search of something more real
than real.
More significant than each minute.
Convincing myself that I had even a modicum of control.
Jesus fuck, we are as naïve
as the day is long.

Inevitably,
regardless of permission or convenience,
your other half kicks the doors in
and pulls you into their arms
unselfishly.

That's the day you breathe.
That's the day you live on purpose.
That's the day you wake with reason.
That's the day you give them the flowers growing all along
from within,
that were only waiting for the right season
to begin.

The Melvin Is Velvet

On their first date
my father told my mother
that she would be his wife one day.
He was crazy in the right ways.
I suppose you know when you know.
Love cares little of convenience.
Just as stubborn as it is blind,
always a bit behind or ahead
of perfect timing.

I've gotten so much of my life wrong,
that I can only ask and hope for forgiveness
when distrusting something right.
Some days I awake with only enough energy
to feel for myself.
Some days,
all I feel is flight.
Until now,
I never understood any of what my father felt,
sitting across from my mother that night.
I exist because of that.
I leave you notes most mornings
because the apple never fell.
I tell you that you will be my wife one day,
knowing all we've gone through,
for this,
only now feels worth it.

Here I sit
drinking alone,
and for once
it isn't to grow numb.
I'm smiling, knowing I will fight to stay.
Drunk enough on us,
accepting that the unknown can be beautiful
and it's only natural, as I'm sure he was,
to be afraid.

Halo

A good friend of a friend
introduced us to her new boyfriend.
He was a bit older,
and wasted little time
leaving a shitty first impression.
After a few drinks,
and listening to him gush about himself
as if anyone gave a fuck,
we all relocated to a gay bar down the street.
The place was packed full of life
and had such great energy to it.
I ordered our drinks, and noticed
upon handing him his
a look of total disgust across his face.

"What's your deal?"

"This fucking place, man....It's vile."

Right then,
a man wearing a sequenced dress and blue wig
prances by,
and the new boyfriend fakes a gag.

"Why the hell is that?"
I ask.

"Listen, I'm all for people being happy and whatnot,
but if one of them tries to hit on me or something
we're gonna have a big problem."

Now I'm the one with a disgusted look.
Which the group recognize immediately
and attempt to mediate.

But there are few things I enjoy more
than the possibility of beating bigotry and homophobia
out of anyone who brags about nonsense like their self-help blog
or small-town fame.

"I'm just saying, it's against my religion. I don't think it's natural. And
I'm a father. I have two boys. I don't want either of them to be
influenced by these types of people."

"How fucking stupid are you? So, your fear is of some hypothetical
scenario, in which a gay man pulls out his cock in front of your kids,
and one or both of them suddenly realize they like the looks of it?!"

He tried to backpedal somewhat,
realizing I wasn't going to entertain or accept his bullshit ideals.
Said that those were just his beliefs,
and that others are entitled to their own.

Why is that ok?
I know that accepting people for who they are
is the "right" thing to do.
But when does **bullying the bully** apply,
if not here and now?

I looked at our friend, told her that it'd be wise
to escort her clown outside, as fast as possible,
before I stomp his empty fucking head in.
And she did.
And a part of me still wishes she hadn't.

They aren't together anymore,
but I still take a little time out of each day
to pray to his God that one or both of his sons
are very happy,
and hopefully
very gay.

Tepid Horizons

Back then,
you had to share bathwater.
The entire family – one tub.
And the dirtiest one went last.
Nobody wanted to soak in their filth,
so one was forced to bathe in everyone else's.

One day,
I will leave this place and move to the woods.
Somewhere far removed and secluded.
Where I am safe from everything trying to kill me.
There will be no police,
no crazed junkies offering me peace,
no news or history,
no women or new memories.

People will write me letters
addressed to a place too inconvenient to visit.
I'll have my four walls and my roof,
my books, my music,
and enough booze to stay warm through the winter.
When I go into town for the bare minimums,
you will not be there.
I'll spend my days fishing,
my nights writing solely for myself.
No one will be there to love, or fuck,
or hate, or fight.
And I'll finally rinse myself clean of everything
I once thought I could not live without.

Foxxxy Scott

There's a group of seven or eight middle-aged men
who gather at the neighborhood bar
nearly every night.
They stand in the back,
playing an arcade style golf game.
The one with the white globe-like trackball you'd spin.
Ten years ago,
I would have criticized and scoffed at them.
Watched and judged their sad little lives,
poked fun at their heated intensity.
"Can you imagine being fifty-something,
and the highlight of your day
is a goddamn bar game?"

I watch them now,
the way they laugh, and celebrate,
throw jabs at one another and clink beers together
when someone hits a good shot,
or wins a few bucks off a buddy.
They give their avatars nicknames like
"Iceman", "Foxxxy Scott",
and
"aPAULcalypse".

They go for hours, and I can only hope that when I'm their age, I have
a similar group of brothers to get drunk and fuck around with.
I'm not sure if any of them have a woman
waiting for their return home,
but I'm guessing with a name like
"OJ Limpson69", his night out with the boys
only gives them both something to look forward to.

Thanks Again

I'm still not certain why we ended, exactly.
Thank you, though.
For reminding me that those closest
are the ones who'll cut you deepest.
You taught me how to let go
before ever being ready to do so.
Proved I could accept apologies owed,
that would never actually be received.

I can still picture you doing lines
while I stood alone in the lobby
searching for somewhere to sleep.
Once I was a thousand miles away,
I wept atop a park bench.
Did you know that?
It's true.
My new lady believes I'm much more
than I actually am.
She makes loving me look easy,
which, for me,
is new.

Now you're here, nearly two years later.
Not one phone call, or single message exchanged
in all that time.
Whenever I see a woman with red hair
I'm reminded of us shooting pool that night.
You were wearing those jean shorts,
I was completely enamored,
and Jesus Christ,
we should have known better.
It's nice to hear from you.
You must have heard I was doing well.
I'm not surprised.
People like you tend to circle back,
somehow sensing when I have finally
moved on.

Reaching out with empty pleasantries
once it's too late,
thinking it safe.
How's your mom?
She still touches base regularly.
Says that she is praying for me.
I told her that it seems to be working,
and to focus more on helping you find some reasoning.

You once said that all you hoped for
was that I would someday be happy.
Well,
seems I took that shit literally.
And I can't begin to tell you how grateful I am
for the way you left me.
I swear,
you gifted me so much hurt
that I had no choice but to make a blessing
from what I only knew previously
to be a curse.

Listen, thanks again for the lesson,
and I hope that you're half as happy.

Certified Pre-Owned

You could lie, cheat, steal,
get hooked on rock or heroin,
and most in your circle would accept that
before they accept your peace and happiness.

"What kind of car do you drive?"
was such an ignorant question
it deserved an ignorant answer.
We are clearly stuck on so many shallow things,
that our superficialities supersede us.

"Oh….it's a two-thousand-fourteen-go-fuck-yourself."

Now I'm the bad guy.
Or, more so, I always was,
only now she knows.
Her wine hits my face,
tastes sweet.
That's life nowadays -
I can't wait to feign an apology,
go Dutch on this tab,
and not call her after we cum a few times tonight.

That was my last blind date.
And had I not been tossed out of that woman's house
in Vegas,
we may not ever have met.
There's no sense doing your head in over this shit.
Yet,
I know too well
will happen anyway.

Kind people are so fucking rare
they seem too good to be true.
We did this to ourselves.
Close friends have traded places with family members
I simply don't care for anymore.

Good music fills the dead spaces
of my most dark and difficult days.
In between all of that,
I find just enough solace writing about why
half of this hell is my fault,
and how you can't seem to realize why
the other half is obviously yours.

I crave empathy so badly
that the only ones I keep around
are reminded over and over again
of how much the world needs them.
We were never rock stars. Just so we're clear.
But certain songs bring me straight back
to San Francisco.
While others drag me home to New Orleans.
Either way,
I'm listening. I'm waiting.
I'm drunk, rambling.
Jumbling random thoughts together
as lessons learned too late,
never caring much whether or not they make sense
to any of you.
Secretly, all the while,
desperately hoping they do.

Foebia

For three days I have been hiding from,
haunted by, and hunting down the most monstrous,
piece-of-shit-asshole-mother-fucking
cockroach that I have ever seen in my life.
This morning….
    we met again.
In the bathroom.
It was there, gnarly as I remember, beside the toilet,
lurking
and plotting my demise.

Half a bottle of Windex,
four shoes
and a vacuum later…

I arose victorious.

He/She/It fought valiantly,
with as much honor as a cockroach could possess.
Drowning the son of a bitch in window cleaner
did nothing but leave it with a shiny, streak-free shell.
While the ammonia only reinvigorated and emblazoned it
like a punch drunk boxer in between rounds.

When it was over, I wept.
I was shaken, trying to calm an unhealthy,
rapid heart rate, filled with equal parts pride
and relief over the realization that I could now,
finally,
take my morning shit in peace.

I am a man.

Save The Elephants

They tell me
"happiness is an inside job".
I'm resting cold hands and a warm heart
atop piano keys of imitation ivory.
Save the elephants.
Save rock and roll.
Save yourself.
I'm well enough.
My muse is one hundred proof.
She hits hard,
punches through tough guts.
Yet, she tastes sweet against my lips,
and gentle to much touch.
I wonder if you'll give me a minute to feel it,
because it'll take some time
for me to believe in any of this.

My cynicism was romanticized for so long
that they will hate hearing I'm at peace.
I still have a lot to say and feel.
Wouldn't it be nice if we all found something real?
To find someone who pinpoints the parts dead
and discarded,
then helps you heal?

Go on then....
project upon me all your doubts and insecurities.
It's time I shook free from so much of what,
for too long,
has been killing me.

Shedding the heaviest weight
means leaving most of what I know,
who I know,
behind,
for better - no worse.

I can no longer look over my shoulder.
Doesn't mean you shouldn't go forward.

Please know that I kept my hope
right where I could find it,
not somewhere the rest of the world
could see it.

The Last 48

"Some of your stuff is just too dark",
she said.
"I guess."
"You should write like you did before."
"I should."
"I bet if you wrote about all the good things in your life,
you would feel better about it."
"Yea, probably."

Then, we just listened to music
until she thought of something else to say.
I never caught much of her points or stories,
though I do remember a line from one song
specifically, which went –

"*your mouth don't move,*
but I can hear you speak",

and I smiled at the irony of timing.

She just continued on,
thinking it was all for her –

my smile,
and all the words.

Gloryholing

Most of the writers are weak these days.
Too attached to the wrong things
not enough hardship and sick living.
The internet has them spayed.
Nearly the whole lot of them are pedaling
T-Shirts and fodder
in the name of cellular fame and a dollar.

I have seen behind their curtains.
I have looked through their empty eyes,
watched them beg and plead for acceptance
and approval.
There is no going back now.
Addicts.
They're already stroked to sleep
by the hands from which they eat.
Their art is compromised, at best.

All we can hope for now
is that they take to a new hobby
or suffer some internal breakdown.
A low so low
where relatability becomes secondary.
Above telling you what you *want* to hear,
exists a brutal truth needing to be shared.
And isn't that supposed to hurt?
But, for many of them,
not being popular is their fucking nightmare.
Not being widely-known and admired
is more than they could possibly stomach or bare.
They are gone to the glory.

But you aren't.
Not yet, at least.
Don't you want your collar wrung?
Don't you want to be shaken awake by something,
anything,
that might not apply to everyone?

I need you to disagree.
Reject me. Hate me.
Spit on my opinions and beliefs.
Just......please,
feel something real.
Entertainment is so cheap these days.
It's a business card. A street sign.
A fortune cookie quote.
Don't give your attention away so easily.
Make us earn it. Challenge us.
Fight us over it.
Call us on trite bullshit being passed out lazily.

Criticize the arts. Denounce it, if you must.
Shake free from the silly drivel you have always enjoyed
and grow.
Lose your rigidity.
Art is not subjective.
Some is good.
Most should be used as dumpster fire kindling.

Be half as insightful as you pretend to be
and we will work on being half as talented
as we pretend to seem.

*Happenstance

See,
I believe more in the energy of two people.

The way they randomly
impossibly
find one another.
Their connection is one more last chance,
a terrifying happenstance,
and above all else -
genuine.
It cannot be ignored
nor contrived.

I am not sure how you ended up here,
yet I do know that I now awake each morning
feeling as if you're the biggest reason why.

I no longer try and make sense of things like this.

Some moments,
some people,
are much too significant for us to understand.

The Coffee Is Ready

I awoke this morning and noticed
I had prepped the coffee pot and set aside two mugs,
from habit.
Funny how quickly those take form.
Like, how unfamiliar it is to simply begin my day
without you.
It starts off all wrong.
The feel is gone.
I smell you on our sheets,
and perfume from your robe hanging off
the bathroom door,
while I brush my teeth.

Time is relative -
the same minutes and hours I lose track of
when you are near,
drag on hellishly slow without you here.
So, I keep busy...
think of things I could say
that might make you laugh.
Tell myself to be sure to remember them
for when you're back home again.
I should write them down.
Just to be safe.
Because my memory isa real bitch, forever deceiving me.

Instead,
I put pen to page and all that ever escapes
are a thousand variations and different ways of saying,
"I love you. You are my hands.
You are my best habit of all. Hurry home."

'Ello Piper

Beautiful fools plan for old age
as if guts and glory exist there.
Forever longing for the unknown.
Wasting away their most fruitful years.
Retirement lands like climax –
short and hardly ever worth it.
I'll take fifty or sixty lived weirdly.
Wildly thorough.
Save the medicine and bedside slippers for those hardly
remembering the names of great grandchildren.
Contentment grows like green grass
always on the other side.
Struggle, save, live within your means
with stagnant discipline.
Forgo anything threatening,
all things life-shortening,
for the sake of longevity and a gold Rolex.
Get that condo in Arizona or Boca Raton.
Cruise your wrinkled ass off until your heart bows out.

The future is currently on sun setting horizons
we work too hard towards,
in the middle of ignored days ransomed by Kings.
Man alive,
arteries and 401K's rarely last long enough, huh?

Squeeze the life out of every slickened minute.
It's all you have for certain.
When my end arrives, I intend to be there fulfilled,
bank accounts depleted, waiting to ask -
"where the hell have you been?"

Monsters Make Masterpieces

You have got to scare the hell out of yourself
and create something excitable.
Strip the ego and familiarity away,
exposing the fiery nerves and bending bones.
Get to the guts of your art.
The terrors, the panic attacks,
the phobias of the heart.
Bury your conventional ways of thinking alive.
Watch it take its final breath
before swallowing that last heavy shovel of dirt,
and do so
whether the world is watching you or not.
Do it.
Do it in a way that others oppose.
Do it defiantly, violently,
wrap your hands around the throat of formality,
until all that remains is your stark, naked truth.

Make music. Share your story.
Sing your life's song.
If you're not offending the status quo
and giving the masses your shoulders to stand upon,
then you're not creating a single thing that this world
can't live without.

The mistake is in believing only "love" is what's
beautiful.
I have seen monsters make masterpieces of the things
that most can't help but run and hide from.

Road Island

Passing through the smallest town
within the smallest state in the country,
most of the men here are beer bloated
and violently vulgar.
The women are raised into razor-wire
guarding a gritty little girl and her few remaining
hard earned dollars.
The white boys drive by drunk
playing that funky music too loudly for anyone listening.

There is an overgrown flowerbox full of mint and basil
that goes ignored,
until I steal an entitled handful from it.
Careful to leave the roots intact for next year.
Every window sill is covered in spider webs,
littered with gnatty frat boys and spineless flies.
I cannot locate the widow,
and shift uneasy atop the barstool
when something brushes against the back of my neck.
We make love so ugly
that it must be art.
There are winners and losers,
and most of us are just waiting our turn to feel one
or the other.

These are gifts.
All of this.
Even when we are most heartless,
death spares us another night.
Life tells us too quietly
that there is still enough left worth living,
that all we can do while learning how to best do so
is fight.

Who You Might Be?

I am low country cemeteries in summer.
An empty matchbook wearing every strike.
I am both love and hate,
and loved and hated.
The hippie bereft of hope, swallowing the parachute.
A creature of bad habits.

I am obsessed with you every morning,
living fast off amphetamine dreams.
The hero of someone else's story.
Folded corners of our favorite pages
in old books we'll never pick up again.

I am the literal cliché,
and Jesus Christ,
it feels damn good.
I am out of tune, out of touch,
left hearing and feeling everything
all at once.
I am excess guitar string for no reason.
A middle finger down your throat,
and also the helping hand extended.

I am begging hipsters to buy my books,
hoping they'll donate it to someone more in need.
I am your blood beneath my fingernails,
signing my name on basement floors
and dive bar bathroom stalls.
I am wasting the little money I owe
to tip every old man playing the harmonica just right.

I am your one night stand,
an orgasm with open arms,
the tobacco-stained mustache you still taste
on your lips,
and everything your daddy said to steer clear of.

I am the guilty bystander.
The dog without leash,
tags,
home
or
owner,
walking down the interstate shoulder,
never recognized in rear view mirrors.

I am both more and less
than what you see.

Forever curious
of whoever the hell you might be.

Spare A Smoke

He offered me a dollar for a spare cigarette.
I declined, told him to just take one.
I don't need the buck.

A bit later,
he offered me five dollars for two.
I accepted that deal.
I'm only generous to a certain extent.

When I walked inside to order another drink,
the bartender asked if I wanted a free margarita.
Said he misheard, and made it by mistake.
I accepted that as well,
though I'm not much of tequila drinker.
I'm only particular to a certain extent.

Some nights, I get lucky.
In spite of my attitude, or karma,
or a daily horoscope.
I don't normally want for anything.
I just accept that it'll all work itself out.

Right or wrong,
bad or good,
that's just the way life goes -
and it's much easier when you don't obsess
over what you believe you're owed.

Cowboy Killers

For two months I chain smoked the same
Red's that ultimately put my father
in an early grave.
He's buried right beside his youngest brother.
I'm a slow learner,
but I now smoke Twenty-Sevens or Lights
A bit less deadly.
Which isn't saying much.
Like all the times I've made sure to buckle my seatbelt
before driving home drunk.
Or wearing a condom half the time,
and pulling out the other half.
Like only mixing my four-cup-a-day coffee addiction
with natural sweeteners.

I'm trying to swap out a few of my worst habits
with some healthier ones.
Though I lack the traits necessary to see most anything through -
ambition, self-discipline, pride,
to name a few.
My grandparents are still kicking about,
while my father and uncle rest cold in Wisconsin.
It all seems like a crapshoot, truly.

As I stand outside the gym this morning
smoking a cigarette,
sweating profusely and catching my breath,
I can only hope that whatever benefits
pain and strain yield,
might one day be worth it.
Worth that one more day.
And that I make something of it.

Still Searching

I would invite you inside
ask you to make yourself at home,
however,
I've been here for quite some time
and have yet to figure out how to do the same.
It's much harder than it looks.
I just realized that I'm more complicated
than I'm often worth.
Too many fall in love with some grand idea of me.
They get sick on my guts,
overindulge on the parts of me fleeting,
unwell by the time they reach the soul and center.

I'm too much.
I'm not enough.

I'm not everything you need.
And I can't figure out why you all continue to
expect that of anyone,
let alone me.
I wonder how many more times you need to
disappoint yourself,
before you realize that the home you are seeking
has never existed
in the ways you're imagining.
It was never a person.
It was never a place.

Home – this peace you and I are searching for,
has always been within a few moments.
I'm still searching for a few more.

Grand Gestures

Judge me as grossly true as I do.
I still remember your burlesque.
That old man splitting his sandwich
with a matted alley cat.
The muddy bayou in my bones.
And the way you tore at my clothes and bags
before hitting the road.
The Stones taught me to feel sympathy for the devil,
so now I feel very little for Kings, Queens,
Presidents,
nor the silver spooned and over privileged.
Take whatever you need.
Fall for the lies.
Believe only in the worst half of me.
Grow cold from what you overlooked.
Hear my stories subjectively.
Our addictions are justified.
Fiends for peace.
My discontent rises to meet you at midnight.

Everlasting – an underdog;
          one who dies naively;
             this is not the life we imagined;
             this is not who we were meant to be.

Climb or crawl up from underneath us, at least.
We're alone.
Like we knew we'd be.
The black list grows long,
another name notched into the bedpost,
we're running out of time and space.
It was good enough
while it lasted.
It lasted long enough
for it to feel worth it.
The next one I slide into
and fall asleep beside

will feel so familiar that I've already
begun carving their name into this wood.

Tonight,
I'll make us dinner,
and in the morning
I'll be sure to make the bed again.
I hope that it's enough,
because we've grown too sincere
for grand gestures.

Deconstructive

Your sobbing rips through sheet rock
like silenced bullets.
I can hear from here
that you'll hate me much more
by morning.
I peek through the holes and watch you walk
down the aisle
wearing ivory.
With each step you take
you smile a bit wider.

Please tell our son only the best of me.

Sorry I couldn't make it.
You must be grateful I can no longer fake it.
Forgive me for always finding the humor
in what isn't yet a tragedy.
With each step you take,
I write another line of the next man's vows
and recite them fraudulently...

"He's the best of men,
and I love the way he loves you both so."

The difficulty lies in attempting to outrun
all of this hurt,
only to stop just long enough to realize
some ghosts haunt from within.
It's great to see you over and over again
in between California and New Orleans.
I'm still wandering mad.
I'm carrying your tears in my pockets
to brand new lands,

trying like hell to erase heavens
burying our remains
which only seem destined to resurface
in the end.

Here I am tonight,
awake with nightmare and photographic memories,
reliving and replaying all of us,
all that was,
all that is.
And I can hear from here
that you'll hate me much more
through the mourning.
This new me is merely a me unworthy
of what I've learned.
This new me is merely a me more adept
at letting go before we're burned.

The old me still exists.
It's what keeps you away
me safe
and hopefully moving closer with each step
towards the best of me
which still persists.

In The Eyes Now

I am finding my way, suddenly.
Learning the streets and dives close by.
Settling a bit more each day
into the idea of us.
Falling foolhardy deep into the reality
of what we are already.
I have yet to unpack anything.
Leave my suitcase open wide
and make myself mostly at home.

My God,
how misguided I've been before this moment.
Before you.
Convincing myself ad nauseam that all of them
were more than unlit lanterns
and mile markers en route to forever –
I'm sorry it took me so long.
I had the earth to scorch.
I've carved this country apart searching
for a heart and mind that might understand
everything I am still learning to say,
breaking both of my own
a hundred times over
along the way.

This was always some sort of dream, to me.
Something I could look forward to
remaining just out of arms reach.
My daddy told me with his eyes
that one day
it would all make sense,
it would be worth all the tears and hurt
in the end.

I wish he was here tonight,
to see for himself how far I've come
just to be happy.
He would have loved the hell out of you, too.
The further I go
and stronger I grow,
the more I seem to resemble him –

in the eyes now,
more so
than ever before.

Relinquishing

We began at the bar.
With you imagining the hand atop your thigh
being wrapped around your throat.
Amidst small talk with strangers,
I leaned in and whispered,
"you're so beyond fucked when we get home",
and you knew me well enough to know
I meant it.

Please check your inhibitions at the door.
There are things you have yet to experience.
Get in the shower.
Do not dry off.
I'll pour us a drink.
Lay down.
Keep your mouth shut.
Everything you say
can and will be used against you.
I am not sorry.
This night will not go gently.
Just go ahead and submit, relax.
You're already arched.
I'll do the rest.
The way you tremble when I kiss your hips
makes me feel pity for anyone who attempts to follow
after this.
The sheets are wet, your body reacts,
I make my way down your spine
to the crook of your back
and you're panting.

I'm in it to ruin you for good.
With eyes closed,
you smirk at ***that*** fact.
Now you're strapped in tight,
wrists and ankles secured.
I tilt your head upward to give you a drink.
You already feel my handprints
my body against yours
me between your thighs.
I turn the music up.
You're fine.
No safe word is necessary.
This is not romance.
This is the furthest thing from what they portray
in movies.
With a fist full of your hair, pulling you into me,
you arch your back a bit more,
and bite your lip to the point of breaking skin.
I kiss you through to the other side of pain.
Where it feels good to hurt.
I shove two fingers down your throat
as you finish,
and I smirk at ***that*** fact.

For us, it's a control thing......
more so
you needing to relinquish it
than me requiring it.
And we succumb to moments few will ever care enough
to know.
Or trust enough to feel.

CatNapped

I find myself in Charlotte.
With a new lady.
It's only May, and I'm on my third relationship
this year.
San Francisco to New Orleans.
New Orleans to Houston.
Houston,
back to New Orleans.
New Orleans to Charlotte.
After the last one
I swore to myself I was going off the grid.
That lasted a month.
Maybe this one is the one which sticks.
She's kind to me, naturally empathetic.
We rarely argue. Usually when I'm drunk.
The biggest issue we have are her two goddamn cats.
They're killing me from the inside out.
No matter how much dusting, cleaning, sweeping
or medications I double-down on
my allergies have me swollen, red-eyed
sneezing and sniveling like a third grader
with snotty sleeves.
I dislodge and hock up dander
from the back of my throat.
Fish hairs out of my morning coffee.
The grocery store clerk smiled and gave me a
"that's what's up" nod earlier today
after seeing my eyes,
convinced I was stoned out of my gourd.
I fucking hate cats. I don't deserve this.
But it's only May.
So I convince myself otherwise.

More Tipsy Than Mystic

I've become so self-aware
that it's impossible for me to entertain
anyone telling me who I am.
Maybe they see me in ways I've already outgrown
to forgive and forget.
I've learned that we only label it
"judgement"
when it's negative.
The rest is praise and flattery,
and we crave it.
To me, it's all the same.
So I ignore all the voices.
When I fall, I fall forward.
Standing myself back up,
never still,
never stalling.
My crashing and burning is so brilliant at times,
that people crane their necks as they pass by.
Stop. Stare.
Pretend to care.
And now that we're nearly done,
there are some things I wanted to share -

mostly gratitude, and yes
some regret.
Please don't chalk us up to stars, or fate,
or some ignorant divinity.
I want to be right, and I need the responsibility.
When we couldn't turn the page
we ripped it out at the spine,
tore it from our guts.
Peace, for me,
is meeting myself at the lowest points,
looking him in the eyes
and accepting that who I am is not who
I will always be.

Pain, for me,
is coexisting with so many others
who run from their vulnerabilities.
The only things left unspoken between us nowadays,
are harsh truths.

I tried to write the last lines of our goodbyes
from the bar.
Promises inverted, reneged,
out of breath.
It came out frantic, bloody, morose,
hyperbolic.
Isn't that this?
How fitting......

Feel free to call me in the future.
Once we've healed,
or no longer give enough of a fuck.
Tell me how far you've come.
Show me your heart, like you did last winter
without fear.
I'm so grateful for us.
I'll still be here.

A Key

There's a key I carry with me always.
Brown and worn down,
decorated with cartoon M&M's.
My son picked it specifically
from the hardware store,
once his mother said it was time I came home.
It no longer opens that same door,
and I haven't seen either of them
in far too long.
Most of the time
it sits in the bottom of my suitcase.
I notice it whenever I'm unpacking,
or repacking
somewhere new.
Which has been far more often than I anticipated.
Some days
I carry it inside my front right pocket.
When I'm most lost,
or alone,
or furthest from him – my home.
I'll walk down the street,
or dig for my lighter,
or fish out spare change for someone in need
and I'll feel for it,
for him – for what could have been.
And I recall how it felt to love and to bleed,
simultaneously.
And one day I'll explain this to him in person -
no matter where I go
he was there,
he was always with me.
A key – closing and opening the parts of me most necessary.

Surf Inn

I have so many torn out pages
from fully-filled notebooks,
that it's safe to assume I hate most of my work
my words
my truths
a hell of a lot more than you ever could.
Thank all things godless for that.
The way I'm able to force feed myself self-awareness,
starve the ego to death,
and allow the world to leech freely off me
whenever it's fitting.

I'm in Nowhere, NC,
at the realest dive I've been to in a long while,
drinking cheap well-whiskey
from a plastic, teal cup.
Using a pink bendy straw to push the uppermost pieces
of ice down to the bottom.
And the last guy who stood up to use the restroom
was harassed by his buddies with a chant of,
"Know your role. Close your holes. Just say no."

Seemed a bit overboard,
but it made me smile.

I could die here
if I wasn't so busy writing about how I should live
more wisely.
The bartender is a beastly broad,
but friendly enough.
One you would know on sight
isn't one to fuck with.
All the regulars are wall art,
bar top fixtures,
with asses so molded into their favorite seats
that it only makes that anyone new who follows
should feel uncomfortable for a while.

This page,
I decide I'll keep.
It won't be ripped from the binding
or tossed into the beer filled trash bin tonight.
It'll be my reality.
The one those I've never met
most likely imagine it to be.
The one I portray so naively.

Tomorrow,
I'll do something else
just as honest
just as sincere.
Only, I'll keep it to myself,

grow further at peace with the fact that some of my words
are words I'm glad you will never hear.

I Wrote You A Letter

We sat on the couch eating sandwiches earlier today.
They forgot Swiss cheese on mine
and mustard on yours.
And that was the extent of it.
The end of any bitching.
A minor inconvenience not worth remembering.
After you left for work
I tried writing you a letter.
Sober.
But it all came out too sweet. Too gentle.
Felt dishonest -
like a me you would never have believed.
Not that I'm a few drinks deep
all my truths come out harsh and unnecessary.
I most likely won't let you read it.
I'm tired of feeling to much of the wrong things,
and not enough of the right ones.
Before you left, you kissed me as if it were the last time.
Told me you loved me in between each
and how much you wished you wished we could just roll around
in bed all day watching tv.

All of that was surely more significant than whatever I'm trying to say.
I wish we would remember that more.
That we rarely find the right words in the moment,
and that sometimes our real life is worth reciting.
I wrote this instead....for you....
hopefully you understand what I mean.

Nearly There Now

When you get wherever you are running from
or towards
send me a letter, please.
Let me know you made it somewhere safely.
I hope summer arrived a bit early.
I hope you're honestly making new memories.
Goddam, I miss your face.
And your scent upon these sheets.
And the way your laugh once saved me.
I know it's best that we no longer speak.
What's worse,
is that I moved myself so far away
in search of space to stretch out
and room outside run and play.

We have both too much
and not nearly enough life left
to waste days killing ourselves over this.
I never meant for us to feel like forever.
We were always just in passing,
another to keep company with when needed.
My intentions were only half as deep
as the feelings turned out to be.
Forgive me for that.
We shouldn't try so hard.
I'm on more solid ground now.
Found myself someone easy.
Who overlooks the worst sides of me.
The same ones you never learned to tolerate.

We're told the answer is "love",
forgetting that, maybe,
we must first learn to question
what it is we hate.

I hope to hear from you again,
some day.
If I don't, though
I'll know you made it to wherever you dreamt of,
and I was merely a stepping stone
along the way.

Somewhere needing to be felt,
and not a place either of us intended to stay.

Ten-Fold

I'm begging for the minute of reprieve I know well
I never earned
and no longer deserve.
The few friends remaining
remind me to hang tight to silver linings -
that I'm someone worth living.

Jesus Christ, no human
no man
should consume as much as I am consuming.
They ask me when the last time was that I spoke to my son…

sixteen months-two weeks-three-days.

I've given the world five years of honesty
now my inbox overflows with cheap flattery
and hate mail insinuating misogyny.
I no longer believe in God.
Saying "Jesus Christ" is hyperbolic – an exclamation at this point.
So, thank you all for that.
Really.
Though I still take time each day to speak to my father,
on the off chance he's still listening.
Let him know that I'm sorry.
That I'm still learning how to be half the man he was,
and ask for advice on what to do with the other half of me
standing in the way.

Is this when the whiskey kicks in?
Is this where the right words begin?
Because I've got things to say,
and my only hope is that I find out how
soon.
In time for a few to hear them.
I continue on, trod along forward,
reminding those closest that one day I will repay them all
ten-fold.

Maybe my only other hope
is that they believe me.
That there's still enough left of me to trust.
I've been called an "asshole" a few dozen times this week,
though its been six years since I was called a liar.

Maybe that's something my father and son
would be proud of.

It's something.

Renegade Bennie

Mixing evenings with antacids
lungs and bellies full,
too much rum and Otis Redding later
we realize that happiness is far more momentary
than monetary.
I rub two nickels together
wearing my smile as a sure sign that my feet
have long since left the ground.

We haven't met everyone who will help define us
yet.
We haven't heard every song which will cure us
yet.
We haven't made our best memories and biggest regrets
yet.

Smoke clouds our vision
tomorrow is too brazen
everything imaginary is worth exploring
milk carton kids forgetting their way back home.
The key is to remain under the weather
and above the ether.
Grow sicker of reality
steal life as if it's all yours
and this moment might actually be our last.

We're rich
just as we are.

*She has the spirt of a mermaid
And a wild heart to swim deep

*Are you thinking?

Ranting #1

If you relate to these types of posts, you likely believe *The Devil Wears Prada* was an instructional video. In between gym selfies, you're probably complaining to your besties that all the good fats from your avocado toast aren't going straight to your lips and it's really thee worst. The last book you read was probably "How to Be a Sexy CEO Bitch & Glittering Girlboss in 90 Days".

I bet you're better informed on the Kardashians and the remaining Bachelorette contestants than you are on Susan Anthony or Maya Angelou, which is totally cool because really, fuck 'em, that new T Swizzle album just dropped in time to remind you that you still deserve the whole entire universe.

Words with sincere depth are tricky little slut bags with brains, gurlz.

But you stay extra savage, make sure every day is sponsored by Cardi B, and never let the fact that you've slept with six different dudes named "Mike" convince you that you aren't a Queen in training, who loves anything mindlessly written that makes no goddam sense but gives you #allthefeels.

*She's so savage that the ocean
respects her heartbeat
And the universe loves her soul

*No it doesn't

Ranting #2

I lay the trite and vapid down to sleep, and pray the internet my hoe to keep. And if I learn one single ignorant thing before I wake, I pray pop culture my soul to take. May God have mercy on those with no dignity, or shallow gag reflexes. Bitter beer face fools with collagen lips and labia reconfiguration on match.com dot cumming to divorced men with greyhound beards soaked in tea tree oil.

If we loved you we wouldda put a cock ring on it, but instead we slid into your DM's like broken home plates, self-perpetuating a generation your greatest grandparents would have coat hangered.

You love this quote, don't you?

You lovely bit of backwash, you.

You remind me of a story my grandmother once told me about a rat who was so much of a rat that at the end of the story, it was a big, fat, dumbass rat, only twenty-five years older. Now I'm forced to weave your whiskers into whiskey folklore, and overlook the fact that many are mostly low-functioning autistic stuck at peace in public rat traps.

Waaaaaiiiiitttttttttttt......

She was a butterfly with broke wings and dreams, flying into suns forevermore and ever after. When "he" breaks you, remember "she" is the one who saved you and made you...uh....more......YOU!

You're a survivor, because anyone who isn't wouldn't buy any of my books. I was told that if I continue to alienate and offend my "fanbase", I would ultimately go broke.

Cheers to going for it. Didn't you know that?

That most of the shit you are reading from anyone NOT ME is mostly choreographed and contrived? Well, now you know what I've always known, and rather than further beg you to support my art, I'll ask you once more for the umpteenth time,

"Are you thinking?"

"Are you using your brain?"

and to please, "Keep growing with me".

Good day to all you wenches and bros on a half shell.

*She was a tidal wave of fierce love
Drowning the world in her dreams

*See also: satire

Ranting #3

Do you read more quotes than literature, or aspire to someday promote and sell fitness tea and start-up clothing companies? Are you finding it increasingly more difficult to hold meaningful FaceTime conversations while wearing teeth whitening trays? Has jogging to The Chainsmokers while selecting the perfect Snapchat filters become an extreme sport, placing our safety and well-being at risk? Do you find yourself looking deeply into your front-facing camera for long periods of time, holding non-existent, make believe conversations with Rhianna and Amy Schumer?

Mirror, mirror, on the wall,

who's the shallowest narcissist of them all?

Was Beauty & The Beast a painful reminder that reading novels are more attractive than hoeing above moon quotes,

or that hairy Bulgarian dude who finger banged you at Bonnaroo?

Fear not, Slow White, you might be one of the millions of self-absorbed pimples suffering from O.V.B. (Overexposure to Vapid Bullshit).

Pretending to be insightful, while trying to calculate the number of oral favors you'll be expected to perform during that paid trip to Dubai, is tough work, but your treatment options shouldn't be.

Ranting #4

'Ello ladies. Have I told you lately how beautifully broken you are? No? My most insincere apologies. Sometimes I forget just how popular nonsensical pandering can be. Book sales have tapered off ever since I stopped lying to you all. An illiterate instapoet told me recently that my "engagement" is lacking, after I #couldnoteven over his trail of verbal dog water which went

"I'll never stop chasing stars. Even if it doesn't bring me closer to the moon, I still feel closer to myself."

How the fuck can I compete with that level of genius? It's so profound that I'm considering dusting off this old resume of mine, and applying to Blockbuster for the fifth time. For the benefits, at least. And free VHS rentals of Love, Actually. For the inspiration, at least.

I'm not bothered by you mermaids half as much as I loathe the mermen force feeding you pseudo feminist fodder, using as few characters as possible. This would all be so much easier if I just went ahead and joined them. I mean, I already have the facial hair, tattoos and typewriter. That's douchey #instapoet 101. I could have a million cackling followers by now, for fucks sake. The male Rupi Cower, without the viral period leak pic. If I would just ditch the pen and page, and text myself she quotes to post alongside sketches of moon flowers or a girl riding bareback atop a shooting star. And hashtags! I need more hashtags, less metaphors, zero punctuation, a Guy Fawkes mask, and meaningless one-liners photographed with dried daffodils which took longer to stage, arrange, filter and post, than it took to contrive. This goddam algorithm is making me want to Love You, But Leave You Wild. Where's a celebrity repost when I need one? Ugh. These sorta rants never help. Some laugh. But the ones who really need to hear it, only end up blocking me from continuing to never follow them.

I'm too old to be a hipster doofus. Too much of a prick to tell you what you want to hear. Too self-aware to pretend we are all so amazing. Too much in love with the art to bastardize it for a few bucks or followers. Too stubborn to overlook the fact that you relate to lies perpetuated by booger eaters. Too tired to take up crocheting. Too hungry to not eat all the food and women. Too lazy to argue why most everything popular is mental elevator music. Too sexy for my shirt. So sexy. Too annoyed by the masses to want to save any of them. Too much Johnny Cash and too little Katy Perry, to explain why those who think reading asinine stardust and ocean quotes, makes them them dumber than the half-man-child-half-Mater who posted it. Too opinionated, fiery, passionate, curious, assertive, alive, aware, well-read, committed (you know, many of the same things you claim to be), to listen to anyone tell me that art is entirely subjective.

Some is good.

Most is god awful.

I may not be the expert, judge or jury on artistic quality and legitimacy, but clearly neither are the masses. Ask yourself WHY you enjoy the things you enjoy. It's ok not to know any better. Just….try.

Question everything. Don't denounce those who simply disagree with you. I dislike most of my own work, after a short time. It's growth. Just because the size of the crowd is increasing, doesn't mean the IQ's of everyone included are as well.

I wasted fifteen minutes that I will never get back, writing this. Simply in an attempt to change the minds of strangers who stopped listening fourteen minutes ago.

Now who's the idiot.

Remember?

Remember when our God was aluminum foil
wrapped around a coat hanger on Saturday mornings?
And love was a punch in the arm?
Adventures were nightly
and memories were scrapped knees.
Forever was a first kiss
and our biggest fears were hidden from
beneath our bed sheets.

Remember our innocence –
when heartbreak and death had not yet shook us
bicycles doubled as round trip tickets
and clouds looked like spaceships and elephants.
Don't you see it?
Just there...

Remember when risks where stepping stones
choking on our first cigarette
too afraid to inhale.
We were petty thieves,
trespassing romantics sneaking anywhere
we weren't allowed.
Always ignorant to everything outside of this minute.
We were in the heart of every moment.

It makes me wonder whether those were better days
or if we were just better that way.

Remember?

These Are Words

Sailor Jerry
our generations' Jesus
pairing dark wood guitars with goddesses into
long naked nights.
Pawn discarded wedding rings
for brass knuckles
and hot-rods across empty sunbaked highways.
Old postcards from Charleston serve as
bookmarks and breadcrumbs,
her holy cross of cold pewter hangs
from my rear-view mirror.
No one behind us
no one up ahead
Creole Godmothers beckon us back to the Bayou,
beg and weep for our muddy rebirth.

All the lonely eyes of men
sunken.
All the blood soaked smiles from women
lure me in.
The sickness is tomorrow,
liquor breath and burgundy lips
on stamped out cigarettes.
Voodoo dolls looking for a few hours of sleep
surrounded by stitched up kin.
We're outcasted vagabonds
afraid of permanence,
long-time lovers of sin.

Haunt-A-Jaunt

Henceforth
all mirror and anything reflective
have been banned.
Our President,
Native to a platelet rich land
with poisonous crops and cheap scalp for sale,
relocates the capital to Sierra Nevada.

Our women have abandoned us
in order to make up their own minds.
Illegitimate children
avoiding alleyway dumpsters
and coat hanger fates
grow into tax deficits
stamping vanity plates.

2RICH4U
GODH8SU
FU ALL
LOVEMYLIE

The dollar is the almighty muse,
and we raise children to worship Saint Cupiditas –
the Patroness of Greed.
Our blood spills green
and our lives have become observing a cinema screen.

We can't turn away from the things we strangle
in the name of fame,
the best of us has lapped us.
Underground lovers of truth survive in shadows,
retelling stories of great-grandparents who once
sang their song in public
and danced madly in these empty streets above us.

Vacant State

Idolize the open space –
the echoed laugh bounces back off the pines,
a woman's breath tells me her life story,
mornings in the middle of nowheres
urging me to live and love with less.
I grow more and more comfortable with the idea
of going missing for good.

A leaf lands in an embankment
right outside my window,
melts and sinks into it.
The bright white snow makes room for it –
embraces it.
I philosophize the moment
as I do with most
and try to find something major in the minor,
some significance in the trivial,
some realness in the space between life and death.

Share a warm bed with me this winter
a drawer and a little closet space for my few belongings,
and when I walk through the front door
remind me what it feels like to be missed.

The words come clumsily,
yet
out here in these nowheres
maybe we won't need them to travel so far
or mean so much.

Barmory

In San Francisco
there's The Geary Club.
With an old-school jukebox safekeeping a limited,
but quality selection of classics.
Never, under any circumstances, play
Sweet Caroline or *Hotel California*.
There's also Zeitgeist. Go early. Sit outside.
Before the hipsters and techies take over.
Order a Bloody Mary. Or a beer and a shot.
And just watch the new age segregation unfold.

In New Orleans
there's Snake and Jakes.
Dark and oppressive, with low ceilings,
and a dog usually wandering around looking for
food and affection.
There's also The Red Door.
It's small, but heavy. And it stinks.
The cockroaches aren't intimidated or skittish,
but the drinks are cheap.
Effective.

In Houston
there's Velvet Melvin
and Dino's Den.
But Velvet Melvin is the better option.
There's no karaoke or trivia night or Wi-Fi.
The food is better than you'd suspect,
given the ambiance.
And the people there are worth observing,
if not knowing.

Jack's Bar in Warren, RI.
One of my favorites, though I wished they'd open earlier
for those who understand there's nothing better to do
at 10 AM.

Same with Surf Inn,
in Charlotte, NC.
It's quite possibly the best dive bar I've ever frequented.
Free gas station-style hot dogs and bar snacks,
with a history that hangs in the air
and cuts through both vomit and urine effortlessly.

There are many others I'd urge you to get drunk in...

Places free of pretention and mixologists.
They remain mostly unchanged,
unsullied,
stubborn in their defiance
and as close to lawless as possible.
They are honest.
The regulars are fixtures.
As much mantelpieces to the establishments
as they are headcases inherently.

A few of them are out of the way,
hard to find, even.
When you're there,
put your phone down.
Shit,
turn it off completely.
Leave the thing at home.
Write. Converse. Drink.
Buy the person seated beside you a round.
And understand that not all change is for the best.
Some things, some people,
resist,
and My God,
they're beautiful for it.

Remember?

Remember when our God was aluminum foil
wrapped around a coat hanger on Saturday mornings?
And love was a punch in the arm?
Adventures were nightly
and memories were scraped knees.
Forever was a first kiss
and our biggest fears were hidden from
beneath our bed sheets.

Remember our innocence —
when heartbreak and death had not yet shaken us
bicycles doubled as round trip tickets
and clouds looked like spaceships and elephants.
Don't you see it?
Just there...

Remember when risks where stepping stones
choking on our first cigarette.
We were petty thieves,
trespassing romantics sneaking anywhere
forbidden.
Always ignorant to everything outside of this minute.
We were in the heart of every moment.
We were the heart of every moment.

It makes me wonder whether those were better days
or if we were just better that way.

Remember?

Well Deserved

I reward myself with a cigarette after every hour
of writing.
Finding motivation in something killing me
might be the best way to sum up the last five years
of my life.
I was never one to seek the limelight.
This whole thing, the miniscule amount of half-fame,
only takes away from creating.
You shouldn't know me.
I shouldn't be your favorite writer.
My words shouldn't save you,
or help you cope,
or inspire in any way.
These are my truths.
Not yours. Not even ours.
Ninety-eight percent of what I pen is dog shit.
The other two percent is merely worth exploring.
I'm filling empty pages with emptier lines,
half the time.
Trying to make sense of how I got here,
why I loathe publicly,
talking myself in and out of giving the world
my worst sides, my flaws,
everything that makes me ugly.
I will say this though -
every day I wake up with this idea
that if I continue to expose all I am not
to all I hope to become,
perhaps my reward will be a life well deserved
and a death which was earned.
The rest is dog shit.

ABOUT THE AUTHOR

Father
Thinker
Observer

"Cynical realism is the intelligent man's best excuse for doing nothing in an intolerable situation."
~ *Aldous Huxley*

"Basically, at the very bottom of life, which seduces us all, there is only absurdity, and more absurdity. And maybe that's what gives us our joy for living, because the only thing that can defeat absurdity is lucidity."
~ *Albert Camus*

"If I lose the light of the sun, I will write by candlelight, moonlight, no light. If I lose paper and ink, I will write in blood on forgotten walls. I will write always. I will capture nights all over the world and bring them to you."
~ *Henry Rollins*

Made in the USA
Middletown, DE
04 January 2026

24822407R00091